AN ILLUSTRATED HISTORY OF
HINDUISM

AN ILLUSTRATED HISTORY OF
HINDUISM

The story of Hindu religion, culture and civilization, from the time of Krishna to the modern day, shown in over 170 photographs

RASAMANDALA DAS
CONSULTANT: PROFESSOR M. NARASIMHACHARY

southwater

This edition is published by
Lorenz Books, an imprint of Anness
Publishing Ltd, 108 Great Russell Street,
London WC1B 3NA; info@anness.com
www.lorenzbooks.com
www.annesspublishing.com

Anness Publishing has a new picture agency
outlet for images for publishing, promotions
or advertising. For more information please
visit our website www.practicalpictures.com

Publisher: Joanna Lorenz
Editor: Joy Wotton
Designer: Nigel Partridge
Illustrations: Anthony Duke
Production Controller: Steve Lang

© Anness Publishing Ltd 2014

Previously published as part of a larger volume, *The Illustrated Encyclopedia of Hinduism*.

PUBLISHER'S NOTE
Although the advice and information in this
book are believed to be accurate and true at
the time of going to press, neither the authors
nor the publisher can accept any legal responsibility or liability for any errors or omissions
that may have been made.

p.1 The BAPS Shri Swaminarayan Mandir, London.
p.2 Palakhi pilgrimage.
p.3 top Shri Yantra.
p.3 bottom Hindu statue.
p.4t BAPS Shree Swaminarayan Mandir, Illinois.
p4b Ganesh in a temple in Karnataka, India.
p.5t The temples of Angkor Wat, Cambodia.
p.5bl A golden statue of Vyasa and Ganesha, Udupi.
p.5br Wheel of the sungod at Konark, Orissa.

PICTURE ACKNOWLEDGEMENTS
Alamy: /© ephotocorp 2; 29b; /© Flame 3t;
/© Tim Gainey 8t; /© ArkReligion.com 8b;
/© Bruce McGowan 10t; /© Dinodia
Images 91b.
The Ancient Art and Architecture Collection:
18t, 30t, 31b, 44t.
The Art Archive: 23t, 34t; /Harper Collins
Publishers 11m, 32b; /British Museum 29t;
/British Library 50t, 89b; /Stephanie Colasanti
55t; /Mireille Vautier 59t.
Vishnu Balgobin: 35b.
BAPS Swaminarayan Sanstha: 11r, 51b, 95t.
Artwork courtesy of The Bhaktivedanta Book
Trust International, Inc. www.Krishna.com.
Used with permission: 9b, 14, 15t, 26b, 39t,
44b, 46bl, 53b, 56t, 57t, 58b, 59b, 61t, 62t, 62b,
64, 67, 69t, 69b, 75b, 77t, 85t, 88b, 90b.
The Bridgeman Art Library: 24t, 31t; © The
Trustees of the Chester Beatty Library, Dublin
10l, 61b; /© National Museum of Karachi,
Pakistan 17b; /British Museum 22t; /© World
Religions Photo Library 23b; /Dinodia 27t;
/The National Army Museum 32t; /© Bristol
City Museum and Art Gallery 33b.
Christians Aware: 82b.
Corbis: /© Lindsay Hebberd 1; /© Gavin
Hellier/Robert Harding World Imagery 3b;
/© Michele Falzone 5t; /© Michele Falzone
/JAI 12; /© Chris Hellier 16t; /© Atlantide
Phototravel 24br; /© Roger Ressmeyer 26t;
/© Adam Woolfitt 28t; /© Stapleton
Collection 30t, 40, 45t; /© Underwood &
Underwood 35t; /© Hulton-Deutsch
Collection 36t; /© Craig Lovell 37bl; /©
Kapoor Baldev/ Sygma 39b; /© Brooklyn
Museum 42b; /© Frédéric Soltan /Sygma
43b; /© David Nicholls 45b; /© Luca Tettoni
47; /© Ivan Volvin/JAI 52b; /© Peter Adams
57b; /© Christie's Images 63t; /© Reuters
70b; /© Amit Bhargava 71b, 79tr; /©
Christophe Boisvieux 76b; /© Piotr Redlinski
83t; /© David H. Wells 84b; /© Brian A.
Vikander 87tl; /© Historical Picture Archive
88t; /© Tony Kurdzuk/ Star Ledger 20b.
Ananta Shakti Das: 63b.
Rasamandala Das: 49t, 60t, 81b, 21t.
Getty Images: /Robert Harding World
Imagery 55b; /Grant V. Faint 74b; /Robb
Kendrick 79tl; /Keren Su 82t; /AFP 86t, 91t;
/John Henry Claude Wilson 86b; /Allison
Michael Orenstein 87tr.
Goloka Books: 18b, 58t, 76t, 89t, 90t.
Hinduism Today: 54t.
ISKCON Educational Services: 38t, 70t, 79b,
80t, 81t.
iStock: 11l, 66t, 72b, 83b, 92.
Bhavit Mehta: 48b, 53t, 71t.
M. Narasimhachary: 25t, 27b, 42t.
Photoshot: /© India Pictures /© UPPA 36t;
/© NHPA 73m; /© Authors Images 93.
Claude Renault: 19b, 41, 43t, 46t, 52t, 54b, 65,
66b, 68t, 68b.
Param Tomanec: 5b, 7m, 13m, 25b, 33t, 48t,
50b, 51t, 56b, 60b, 72t, 73l, 73r, 78b, 80b, 85b.
Werner Forman Archive: 28b; /Edgar
Knobloch 19t.

CONTENTS

AN INTRODUCTION TO HINDUISM

Hinduism is the oldest living religion in the world. Although it clearly goes back at least 5,000 years, it is difficult to say precisely how it began. Hinduism reveres no singular founder, doctrine or scripture. It has no definite starting date. Throughout its long history, many founders and scholars have taught different philosophies through thousands of texts. To explain Hinduism's diversity, many authors describe it as 'a family of religions' and, for its lack of stress on belief or creed, as 'a way of life'.

This book gives an overview of Hinduism's history from the Vedic Period and North Classical Age through to the Mughal Empire, migration to the colonies and Indian partition. It describes the major holy texts, the Ramayana, the Mahabharata, the four Vedas and the Bhagavad-gita or Song of God, and Hinduism's teachings about the self, the law of karma, and the cycle of birth and death. All significant historical events in 'Sanatana Dharma', the eternal religion, are covered from the time of Krishna to the birth of Guru Nanak, founder of the Sikh religion, the assassination of Mahatma Gandhi and the role of global Hinduism today.

Opposite: Like this sacred banyan tree, Hinduism has old and deep roots, and has grown organically over several millennia.

Above A sadhu reads the Ramayana, one of two Hindu epics. This ancient wisdom, the Sanatana Dharma (eternal law), was first transmitted orally.

THE ORIGINS OF HINDUISM

HINDUISM IS A RELIGIOUS TRADITION THAT DEVELOPED OVER SEVERAL THOUSAND YEARS. ITS HISTORY IS INEXTRICABLY ENTWINED WITH THE POLITICAL AND SOCIAL DEVELOPMENT OF INDIA.

The noun 'Hinduism', denoting a distinct, unified religion, was first coined by the British in the 19th century. Around the 8th century CE, Persians first used the adjective 'Hindu', broadly indicating the people beyond the River Indus.

Some people identify Hinduism with its stereotypical images: its many deities, the revered cow and the saffron-clad ascetic; others associate it with Indian poverty and the caste system. Some try to define it by identifying distinctive beliefs, such as karma and reincarnation. Others highlight its spiritual practices, such as yoga, worship and meditation.

Historically, Hinduism is linked to geographic India: her tropical climate, her fertile river plains and her vulnerable north-west frontier. In the modern era, especially since the partition of India in 1947, Hinduism has become a truly global religion.

Right A decorative 'Om', the sacred syllable used to represent the family of traditions now called Hinduism.

HISTORY

Trying to pinpoint Hinduism's origins is perplexing. Followers claim their tradition goes back indefinitely to previous 'glorious ages'. Standard texts date recent history to the onset of the present age, called the Kali-yuga (age of quarrel), coinciding with Lord Krishna's departure from the world 5,000 years ago. Modern scholars often cite more recent dates, believing that Hinduism emerged somewhere between 1900 and 1500BCE.

Accepting the Aryan invasion theory, early European intellectuals favoured the view that Hindu ideology came from beyond the subcontinent, from Europe or Central Asia. The hypothetical Aryans prevailed either by conquest or, it was later thought, by migration and cultural infiltration. Many Hindus argue that Hinduism has always been indigenous to India and often reverse the colonial interpretation by promoting India as 'the cradle of civilization'. These debates, fuelled by ethnic bias, may never be resolved. Nevertheless, the history of Hinduism is intimately linked to India's early civilizations, her domination by foreign powers and, more recently, national independence and global migration.

Left Shiva and the Ganges. Hinduism is also called the Sanatana Dharma (eternal religion). It teaches of an eternal reality and a repeatedly created material world, overseen by Lord Shiva and other deities.

SACRED TEXTS

Throughout history, most Hindus have located the core of their tradition within specific sacred texts, the Vedas and their corollaries. For this reason, Hindu orthodoxy has distanced itself from traditions that reject the Vedic authority, including Jainism and Buddhism. Orthodox texts are divided into two sectors, the Shruti ('that which is heard') and the Smriti ('that which is remembered'). The Shruti, consisting of the four Vedas, is the main canon, supported and explained by the Smriti, which includes moral codes, the Epics, the Puranas, and a wide range of supplementary literature.

In ancient Sanskrit, Veda means 'knowledge', implying acceptance of universal truth. This inclusive idea has allowed Hinduism to accommodate texts only indirectly connected to the Vedas, provided they support Vedic conclusions. These encompass many Tantric texts (Tantras) often shared with other religions such as Jainism, Buddhism and Tibetan Bon. The Tantric texts are specifically favoured by the Shramana, renouncer traditions, which have complemented the orthodox, brahmin-led religion called Brahminism.

Despite the current use of written texts, ancient Hindu wisdom was first passed down orally. Some Hindus believe oral transmission remains the only legitimate system, especially for the Shruti. Most scholars date the compilation of the first text, the Rig Veda, to around 1000BCE.

HINDU TEACHINGS

Belief in Veda as 'knowledge' does not confine truth to a single 'faith' or creed. Hinduism has largely managed to blend faith commitment with philosophical thought. None the less, most Hindus share distinctive core concepts, such as the notion of Brahman, the eternal reality. Brahman is first understood by apprehending the eternal self (atman), which trans-migrates through all species of life and attains ultimate salvation in union with God.

The Vedic teachings do not mention 'Hinduism' but refer instead to dharma, or 'religious duty'. The term implies preference for regulating practice rather than belief. More precisely, dharma means

Below This depicts the widely accepted Hindu worldview of an eternal self rein-carnating throughout numerous species.

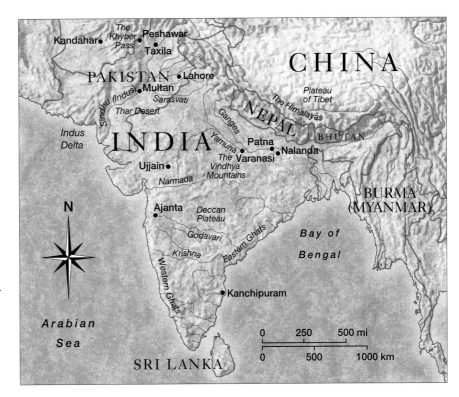

Above Hinduism has been nurtured largely in India. This map shows the main geographical features of 'the subcontinent'.

'duties that sustain humans according to their intrinsic nature'. There are two main types. First, sanatana-dharma, duties that revive the eternal relationship between the soul and God. Second, varnashrama-dharma, or duties based on the eternal self's specific station in life, defined within four *varnas* (social classes) and four *ashramas* (stages of life). While acknowledging spiritual and social inter-dependence, Hinduism also recognizes individual autonomy through its well-known doctrine of karma (moral accountability).

Based on the idea of Brahman, Hindu texts indicate an eternal, indestructible realm. They also describe the material world as ever-lasting, through a cyclical process of creation, destruction and re-creation.

Texts, while accepting the earth as but one planet, describe many populated worlds, stratified levels of reality, and vast stretches of time and space. Although India is just one region of a single planet, Hindus consider India to be sacred, a land sanctified by saints and avataras (divine incarnations). For nurturing spiritual awareness, it is central to the purposes of material creation. This creation is born of the sacred syllable Om, whose visual form is now often used to represent Hinduism.

TIMELINE

HINDUISM'S HISTORY IS COMPLEX AND HARD TO TRACE. IT CAN BE DIVIDED INTO SEVEN MAIN PERIODS, BEGINNING WITH ITS PRE-HISTORY AND THE SUBSEQUENT VEDIC PERIOD, STARTING AROUND 1500BCE.

C.3000BCE–1150BCE

- c.3000BCE According to Hindu tradition, Krishna appears on earth and speaks the Bhagavad-gita just before the start of the Kali-yuga (the age of quarrel).
- c.2500BCE The great cities of the Indus and Sarasvati valleys are at the height of their power.
- c.1500BCE According to Western scholars, the foundations of Hinduism are brought to India from outside by the Aryans.

C.500BCE–500BCE

- c.1500–500BCE During this 'Vedic period', the Vedas are composed in Sanskrit. Focus is on the sacred fire ceremony, reaching the ancestors in heaven, and deities representing the forces of nature.
- c.1200BCE Writing of the Rig Veda.
- 500BCE Sixteen kingdoms extend across northern India.

Below According to tradition, Krishna spoke the Bhagavad-gita prior to the present age, called the Kali-yuga.

500BCE–500CE

- c.500BCE–500CE Buddhism spreads through India. Among Hindus, puja (worship of the murti) becomes popular. Vishnu, Shiva and Shakti as the main deities with their corresponding traditions. The Epics (the Ramayana and Mahabharata) and the Puranas are written.
- 327BCE Alexander the Great invades India, defeats King Porus and confronts the great Magadha Empire.
- 326BCE–184BCE The Mauryan Empire unites much of India. King Ashoka patronizes Buddhism.
- 320BCE–550CE The reign of the Gupta dynasty, a golden and classical age for Hindu arts.
- c.300BCE–300CE The Sangam literature, the earliest known Tamil literature, is compiled (though its oral roots may be much older).

Below An image of Shiva, one of the three main Hindu deities that emerged shortly after 500BCE.

Above This statue of the goddess Lalita dates from the 11th century when temple construction flourished in India.

500CE–C.1200CE

- 500–1000CE The poet-saints of South India compose devotional poems in the Tamil language.
- 535–700CE Rise of the Harsha Empire, uniting much of northern India.
- 550CE Collapse of the northern Gupta Empire.
- 800–1200CE Temple building flourishes, especially in southern India.
- 800CE Shankara teaches that God is everywhere. He re-establishes the importance of the Hindu holy books and formalizes the Smarta tradition. Subsequently, Buddhism declines further in India.
- 1000CE Abhinavagupta writes his Tantraloka, the basis for important Shaiva and Tantric traditions.
- 1000CE Muslim incursions into northern India escalate, with brutal raids by Mahmud of Gazni.
- 1010–1200CE The Chola Empire further extends Hinduism to Indo-China and Indonesia.
- c.1050CE Ramanuja extends Shankara's teachings, advocating that God is a person, living beyond this world.
- c.1140CE Construction of temple complex at Angkor Wat.

Above The Taj Mahal in Agra, India, epitomises the significant social and cultural influence left by the Mughal empire.

Above The period of British domination of India was marred by the Indian Mutiny, as shown here by an English artist.

Above The modern BAPS Swaminarayan Temple, New Delhi, exemplifies the continuing popularity of Hinduism.

1200–1750

- 1200–1500 Muslims become powerful in the north, but Hindu kingdoms flourish in the south, especially the Chola Empire.
- 1238 Birth of Madhva, founder of the Dvaita (dualism) Vedanta school.
- 1469 Birth of Guru Nanak, founder of the Sikh religion. Many devotional saints, such as Chaitanya, Mirabai and Tukarama, live during this period.
- 1469 Birth of Vallabha, who started the Pushti Marg ('path of nourishment').
- 1486 Birth of Chaitanya, charismatic saint and founder of the Bengali Vaishnava movement.
- 1526 The Mughal Empire is founded in India.
- 1556–1605 The liberal reign of Akbar.
- 1600s Many Europeans arrive in India to trade in cloth and spices.
- 1627–1680 The life of King Shivaji, who resisted the Mughals.
- 1632 The Mughal emperor Shah Jahan builds the Taj Mahal as a memorial to his wife.
- 1668–1707 The reign of Aurangzeb, the last great Mughal emperor, who destroyed many Hindu temples.

1750–1947

- 1757 Robert Clive wins the Battle of Plassey, bringing India under British domination.
- 1828 In response to European thought, the Brahmo Samaj is founded as one of many organizations seeking to reform Hinduism.
- 1830 onwards Many Hindus migrate to Fiji, Malaysia, Mauritius, the Caribbean, East Africa and South Africa.
- 1857 Army rebellion during the Indian Mutiny, which many Hindus now call 'the first war of independence'.
- 1858 India becomes part of the British Empire, as the Mughal Empire finally expires.
- 1869 Birth of Mahatma Gandhi, leader in the struggle for Indian independence.
- 1877 Queen Victoria proclaimed Empress of India.
- 1897 Ramakrishna Mission established in Calcutta by Swami Vivekananda.
- 1942 Gandhi starts the 'Quit India' movement.
- 1947 India gains independence, but loses territory to the newly created West and East Pakistan.

1947–PRESENT DAY

- 1947 Nehru is inaugurated as India's first prime minister.
- 1948 Assassination of Mahatma Gandhi at Birla Bhavan, New Delhi.
- 1950s–1970s Hindus migrate to North America, the UK and other countries, such as Holland and Australia.
- 1960s Indian thought and practice become popular in the West, through groups such as the Transcendental Meditation and Hare Krishna movements.
- 1966 Appointment of Indira Gandhi as first female prime minister of India.
- 1984 Assassination of Indira Gandhi causes rifts between Hindus and Sikhs.
- 1992 Destruction of the Babri Mosque precipitates violence between Muslims and Hindus.
- 2000 Continuing strife between Christians and Hindus over coerced religious conversions, especially in Orissa and Kerala.
- 2000 Hindus are socially, academically and economically well-established in the West. With the rise of the Indian middle class, vast temple complexes also flourish in India.

CHAPTER 1

HINDU HISTORY

In exploring any faith tradition, students usually ask 'when did it start?' and 'who founded it?' For the Hindu tradition, such questions yield no easy answers. Most historians consider Hinduism not a divergent expansion from one key event, but a convergence of many spiritual and cultural influences. Many Hindus themselves consider their wisdom eternal. In their view, time is boundless and cyclical, and space similarly extends beyond human perception.

Students of Hinduism often consider its scope and complexity problematic. Although the religion is hard to grasp, its multiformity has also been enriching. Indeed, its fluidity may have helped it prevail for more than five millennia, to become the world's oldest existing religion.

Hinduism is inextricably linked to the recorded history of India. Its vision has long transcended the particularities of a specific era and locale. In practice also, millions of Hindus now live beyond the sub-continent. People of other ethnic origins have adopted elements of Hindu thought and practice. The history of Hinduism, though running parallel to Indian history, is also different from it.

Opposite The Angkor Wat temple in Cambodia symbolizes an era of cultural expansion for Hinduism.

Above A giant wheel of the sun-god at the Konark Temple, Orissa. Ancient Hindu deities acknowledged human dependence on God and nature.

TRADITIONAL VIEWS ON ANCIENT HISTORY

HINDUISM IS THE WORLD'S OLDEST LIVING RELIGION, GOING BACK AT LEAST 5,000 YEARS. ACCORDING TO ITS OWN CYCLICAL WORLDVIEW, IT GOES BACK MUCH FURTHER, EVEN INDEFINITELY.

There are different accounts of Hinduism's early history, for three main reasons. First, Hinduism is not a single, unified religion, with a common founder, but embraces many distinctive branches. Second, there are differences of opinion, especially between Hindu practitioners and Western researchers, who hold variant views on what constitutes authentic research and evidence. Third, Hinduism is so old that its past recedes into uncertainty.

Some Hindus claim that their heritage regresses indefinitely. This distinctive view of time, and the allied idea of a hierarchical universe, clash with much contemporary

Below Lord Rama's triumphant return to Ayodhya illustrates Hindu belief in previous glorious ages.

opinion. However, if one is to study Hinduism thoroughly, to grasp the meaning behind its diverse practices, it is essential to explore Hinduism's own views on time, history and its own evolution.

ETERNAL, CYCLICAL TIME

Many Hindus call their tradition 'Sanatana Dharma' (the eternal religion'). Derived from the core concept of Brahman, the absolute reality, the term implies the existence of an eternal realm. However, the concept of an ever-receding past and an indefinitely extending future also applies to the transient material world. Hindu texts teach of a continuous cycle of universal creation, destruction and re-creation. Time is eternal and cyclical rather than bounded and linear.

UNDERSTANDING HINDUISM

Hinduism's age and complexity, and its own view of time, befuddle attempts to describe its development. The lack of a founder, or single historical event, implies that it is not like dropping a stone on to water, creating successive waves of development. Some have proposed a longer-term analogy, of a tree growing out of the ground and dividing into branches and sub-branches. This still suggests a divergent growth, sprouting from a single base. Others view Hinduism to the contrary, as the convergence of diverse spiritual, social and political influences, citing the analogy of many tributaries feeding into a single river. Other scholars have likened Hinduism to a family of religions, with each distinctive lineage bearing some family resemblance. Clearly, Hinduism fails to resonate with rigid or simplistic notions of religion or with ideas of unidirectional human emergence from a tribal and primitive past.

Since the creation of this universe, time has moved through successive cycles of four ages. Similar to the four seasons, they continuously repeat themselves. They are named after four metals, suggesting the gradual debasement of human virtue. During the golden age, all people were noble. Good qualities decreased through the silver and copper ages until we reached the present materialistic age, called the Kali-yuga, the age of iron. It is also called the 'age of hypocrisy' or the 'age of quarrel'. Hindu texts elaborate on the materialistic qualities prevalent in this age, and the exalted virtues of previous 'yugas'.

There are two Hindu 'histories', taking the form of long poems and popularly called 'the Epics'.

Left Krishna and Arjuna sound their conch shells to start the cataclysmic Battle of Kurukshetra.

or to oppose them, kings from throughout the known world prepared for battle at Kurukshetra, just north of modern New Delhi.

Just prior to hostilities, Lord Krishna – a key Hindu deity – narrated the Bhagavad-gita to the third Pandava brother, called Arjuna. Though a bold warrior, Arjuna was depressed at the prospect of battle with his own kinsmen. Krishna instructed him on all the important Hindu teachings, starting with the idea that the true self (the atman) is different from the physical body. Hearing Krishna's instructions, Arjuna regained his composure and fought with determination. He and his brothers emerged victorious, regaining the throne of the Indian Empire. Krishna departed the world 36 years later, marking the start of the present age.

Below Map showing India's seven holy rivers, seven ancient cities and some sites mentioned in the two Hindu epics, the Ramayana and the Mahabharata.

Some scholars consider them fictional or mythological. They are certainly not ordered chronologically, and it appears that early Indian authors had little concern for history as we know it, the systematic and chronological classification of facts. Despite this, the Epics may give a peep into Indian history, and the progression of Hindu thought, practice and culture. The first epic, the Ramayana, tells the famous story of Rama and Sita, which may have happened as far back as the silver age. The second, the Mahabharata, 'the history of greater India', is more clearly linked to known human history.

THE KALI-YUGA
According to tradition, the Mahabharata recalls the final centuries of the previous era, the copper age. It relates the saga of five princes called the Pandavas, 'the sons of Pandu'. King Pandu was a descendant of King Bharata, after whom India is still called 'Bharatavarsha' (the land of Bharata), or simply 'Bharata'.

The Pandava's avaricious cousins, the Kauravas, usurped the throne of the vast Indian empire. After much intrigue, and extended appeals for peace, the Kauravas refused to give up any of their illegally occupied territory. To support the pious Pandavas,

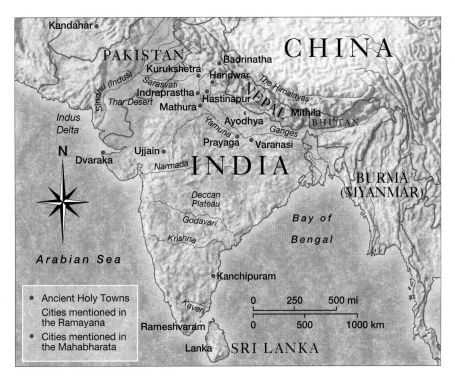

ARYAN INVASION THEORY

IN THE MID-1800S, WESTERN SCHOLARS BEGAN TO EXPLAIN THE EMERGENCE OF HINDUISM THROUGH THE ARYAN INVASION THEORY. IT HAS LONG BEEN CONTESTED, ESPECIALLY BY HINDUS THEMSELVES.

At the core of the Aryan invasion theory was the view that key elements of Hinduism developed outside of India. Critics, on the other hand, have long claimed that the theory is based on conjecture, political agendas, and dubious interpretation of linguistic and archaeological evidence. More positively, construction of an Indian history has highlighted the subjective and political dimensions of research and scholarship. Accounts of Indian and Hindu history were constructed largely during the European colonial period, influenced by prevalent and emergent ideas on

Below Map of excavation sites in the Indus and Sarasvati valleys. The legendary Sarasvati may have followed the course of the current Ghaggar-Hakra river.

the nation state and the pre-eminence of Western and Christian civilization. From the late 20th century, religious scholarship changed, to promote the importance of not only gathering sound data, but also of recognizing factors that skew its interpretation. The broad consensus today is that the Aryan theory is questionable, although many books habitually present its claims as incontestable fact.

LINGUISTIC THEORIES

The first Europeans to arrive in India knew little of Hinduism's origins. They found few historical records, for Hindu writers seemed uninterested in mere chronological accounts. Serious scholarship began during the days of British domination of India, with the development

Above Max Müller, the German Indologist usually credited as the first to propound the Aryan invasion theory.

of the study of philology (the science of language) and Indology (Indian studies), especially in Great Britain and Germany. Early scholars studied religious accounts of history, such as the two Epics, but considered them largely mythological and thus unreliable. In the very earliest text, the Rig Veda, information about the lifestyle and habitat of their authors was largely incidental.

However, scholars observed that Hindu scripture denoted certain people as 'aryan'. Although this Sanskrit term means 'noble people', academics hypothesized that it referred to a distinct race. At the same time, early philologists identified clear links between Sanskrit and European words, and, based on linguistic evolution, tried to construct an historical framework. In 1853, the German linguist Max Müller proposed that the highly advanced Aryans came from outside India, from the West, bringing with them the ancient Indo-European language of Sanskrit and the seeds of Hinduism.

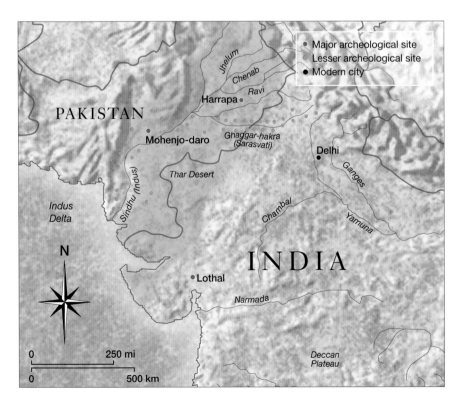

Left This ancient street, unearthed at Harappa, Pakistan, is lined with brick dwellings that housed c.5,000 people.

ARCHAEOLOGICAL EVIDENCE

At first, little was known of the proposed Aryan people. Then, in the 1920s, archaeologists unearthed the remains of two walled cities, Mohenjo-daro and Harappa, in present-day Pakistan. Evidence revealed detailed town planning, with kiln-fired bricks, orderly streets and sophisticated sewage and drainage systems. Clay seals unearthed from the sites revealed an elementary form of writing, although experts have yet to decipher the script. One seal carries a figure resembling Lord Shiva, a contemporary Hindu deity. Scholars were taken aback at the level of civilization shown and its sophistication. Even more surprisingly, the inhabitants seemed to have lived well before the Aryans, then considered the most advanced race of their time.

REVISED THEORIES

Rather than rejecting the original theory, scholars revised it. As an alternative theory to the conquest of an aboriginal people by the civilized, light-skinned Aryans, archaeologist Mortimer Wheeler advocated that the bellicose Aryans had plundered and destroyed the cities of the older, more advanced Indus civilization. What we called Hinduism, he claimed, was a fusion of Aryan belief with the sophisticated culture of the local, dark-skinned Dravidians. The term Dravidian still refers to the peoples of South India.

More recently found artifacts imply that the Indus valley civilization was more widespread than first imagined. Sites extend a thousand miles, making it unlikely that they were simultaneously abandoned with the intrusion of nomadic tribes. Ideas have been refined, so that migration and acculturation, and not military conquest, explain the Aryan infiltration of north-west India, probably around 1700BCE. Recent photographic evidence has enhanced the debate, by supporting the existence of the legendary River Sarasvati, frequently mentioned in the Rig Veda. This implies that the river was not entirely mythological, as earlier thought, and that Hindu accounts of history might be taken more seriously. Hindus texts, however, fail to mention an Aryan invasion. They conversely indicate a protracted westerly migration, carrying Hindu thought and culture to Greece and beyond.

ONGOING DEBATES

Many scholars now seriously consider the possibility that Hinduism developed entirely within the sub-continent. Some even refer to India as the 'cradle of civilization', an alternative to Central Asia or Europe. However, the debate remains politically charged, with Hindu nationalists mirroring their past colonial adversaries. They promote the supremacy of the ancient Indo-Hindu civilization, putatively well-versed in science, medicine and mathematics even as the West languished in fur-clad barbarism. Despite such possibly biased and over-stated claims, contemporary scholars are happier to reconsider previous theories. Many use the wider term 'the Indus-Sarasvati civilization' and entertain earlier dates, more consistent with Hinduism itself. Despite this convergence, conclusive establishment of the origins of Hinduism remains unlikely. Dates and events become relatively clear only as the first millennium CE approaches.

Below Found at Mohenjo-daro in the Indus Valley, this terracotta seal depicts a figure resembling Lord Shiva.

THE VEDIC PERIOD 1500BCE–500CE

THE VEDIC PERIOD IS THE ERA OF INDIAN HISTORY DURING WHICH THE VEDAS WERE COMPILED. IT IS MARKED BY SACRIFICIAL MODES OF WORSHIP DIRECTED TOWARD MANY 'NATURE' DEITIES.

Scholars suggest that these earliest Hindu texts represent the fusion of two cultures: the Aryan and Dravidian. Apparently, Aryan culture predominated, reaching the fertile Gangetic plain around 1000BCE and later infiltrating the southern peninsula. Some scholars claim that the disparity between the Aryan and Dravidian societies, particularly as defined along racial lines, has been over-emphasized. Whatever the precise history, the decline of the Indus-Sarasvati civilizations from around 1900BCE marks the beginning of the Vedic age, which roughly spanned the ten centuries from 1500 to 500BCE.

COMPOSING THE VEDAS

Although India's distant history is uncertain, its ancient wisdom was certainly passed down orally and later committed to writing. Some traditionalists still believe that the Vedas themselves should only be transmitted orally and never through written text. Scholars believe that these first books were composed around 1200BCE, starting with the Rig Veda.

Below An artist's impression of the ancient and grand fire sacrifice, often patronized by wealthy kings.

Above An 11th-century carving of Agni, god of fire, who was especially popular during the Vedic period.

BRAHMIN-LED SOCIETY
The priestly class of the Vedic period were the brahmins, whose prime responsibility was to preserve tradition, originally through oral recitation and later through written texts. They formed the head of what is now known as Brahminical Hinduism, which valued social orthodoxy and family tradition. During the same period, there were early developments of the less orthodox and sometimes anarchical 'Shramana' traditions, whose members lived in forests and remote regions, practising meditation and asceticism and favouring alternative Tantric texts. Scholars suggest that Hinduism consists of these two competing but complementary strands, augmented by the simple folk traditions associated with village Hinduism.

Right The 16 'ancient kingdoms' stretched from modern Afghanistan in the west to the Ganges Delta in the east.

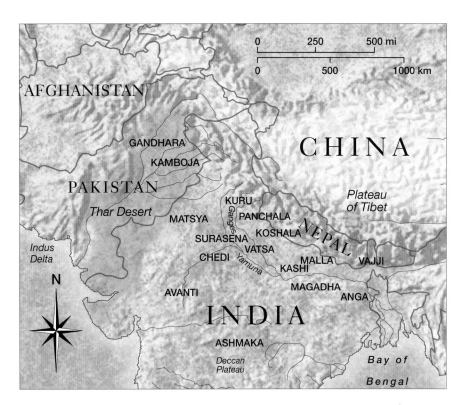

Veda literally means knowledge. Although it refers to a specific body of texts of largely India origin, it carries connotations of a universal wisdom, common to all people. This helped foster notions of an inclusive religion, which valued and assimilated diverse scholarly and cultural influences. The adjective 'Vedic' means 'related to the Vedas'. For this reason, this period is called 'the Vedic age', and the associated culture centred in northern India, 'the Vedic civilization'.

There are four main Vedas, classified as shruti, 'revealed knowledge'. They formed the basis for hundreds of later elaborations, alternatively designated as smriti, 'remembered knowledge'. Together, these two types of holy book are often called 'the Vedic literature'. The Vedas proper included hymns and chants for use in sacrificial rituals, and later philosophical sections called the Upanishads. Over the Vedic period, the importance of ritual gradually diminished as priority shifted to philosophical thought based on the Upanishads.

WORSHIP

The Vedas are primarily liturgical texts for use in ritual and worship. During the Vedic age, the performance of elaborate *yajnas* (sacrifices) aimed at worldly fulfilment and the

attainment of heaven. The sacrifices involved not only the immolation of animals but, more frequently, the offering into fire of clarified butter (ghee) and raw, whole grains such as rice and barley. There were two main types of sacrifice: public events, which included the sacred fire and the coronation ceremonies, and domestic rites, including sacraments for initiation, marriage and death.

Because the Vedas emphasized the need to live in harmony with natural and cosmological rhythms, called rita, the main deities were linked to nature. Most eminent were Indra, god of rain and 'king of heaven', and Agni, who presided over the sacrificial flames and first received the offerings. Soma, supervising the celestial moon planet, was associated with drinking a heady nectar distilled from the enigmatic Soma plant. Vishnu, and Shiva in his form as Rudra, were also venerated, but

Left A Hindu woman daubs sacred clay on her forehead by the banks of the River Yamuna. Most Vedic deities predominated over nature and the elements.

some claim they were relatively less popular deities. Other deities included Usha, goddess of the dawn, Varuna, god of the waters, and Goddess Sarasvati, associated with speech and the sacred river.

HINDU KINGDOMS

By the Vedic period, the noble Aryans had developed an aristocracy based on the varna system. They divided society into four occupational classes. The members of the highest varna, the brahmins, performed rituals and taught from the Vedic texts. They relied on patronage and protection from members of the second varna. These chivalrous kings were addressed as Maharaja (great king) or Mahajana (great man). During the late Vedic era, there emerged several powerful Hindu kingdoms, called 'mahajanapadas'. By 600BCE, 16 realms spanned the Indian plains, from modern-day Afghanistan in the west to beyond the Ganges delta in the east. They paved the way toward the great Mauryan Empire and the dawn of the classical age of Hinduism.

WORSHIP IN THE VEDIC PERIOD

WORSHIP IN THE VEDIC AGE WAS TYPIFIED BY THE PERFORMANCE OF SACRIFICE, CALLED YAJNA. MANY OF THE VENERATED DEITIES WERE ASSOCIATED WITH THE MANAGEMENT OF THE UNIVERSE.

The Vedic Age corresponds to the period of compilation of the Vedas, the oldest texts of Hinduism. Scholars locate it approximately between 1,500 and 500BCE, and the culture prevalent during that thousand-year period is called the Vedic civilization. The mode of worship was performance of yajna, or sacrifice, which included the chanting of Rig Vedic verses, singing of hymns and recitation of mantras. The priests executed rituals for the three upper social classes (varnas), strictly excluding members of the fourth, shudra, class. Members of these upper varnas offered sacrifice for an abundance of rain, crops, cattle, and sons, and for gaining access to heaven. Stay in the celestial realm could be prolonged indefinitely by descendants who regularly performed the appropriate yajna. Such practices were underpinned by the notion of rita, 'the natural order', presided over by numerous deities in charge of nature's functions. They were collectively called the Vishve-devas (universal gods).

INDRA AND AGNI

The Vedic deities were placated mainly though the sacred fire ceremony, in which offerings of ghee (clarified butter) were first received by Agni, the fire god. Of similar stature was Indra, god of rain, king of heaven, and much celebrated for slaying with his thunderbolt a huge demon called Vritra. Other deities were intimately connected to the elements, including Vayu, lord of air, and Varuna, lord of the waters. Many of these deities have entered the contemporary pantheon, usually as minor gods. Cosmological accounts

Above A painting of Indra, c.1700, one of the two main deities during the Vedic period.

suggest that the Vedic deities resided in the heavenly material worlds, and their positions were not entirely stable. Later there emerged the notion of an eternal transcendent realm, reserved for major deities such as Vishnu and Shiva.

PLANETARY DEITIES

Soma was a ritual drink important among the early Indo-Iranians, and the later Vedic and Persian cultures. The hymns of the Rig Veda frequently eulogize its energizing qualities. It was prepared by pressing juice from the stalks of a certain mountain plant, which has not been conclusively identified but has hypothetically been linked to mead, honey, alcohol, cannabis, blue lotus, pomegranate or psychedelic mushrooms. Soma was also personified as a deity, associated with the moon, and 'Soma' remains an alternative name for the moon deity, popularly called Chandra. Some scholars suggest that soma juice,

Left Replicating the ancient Vedic sacrifice, two Hindu priests kindle the sacred fire, representing Agni, before a wedding ceremony in New Jersey, USA.

Above A contemporary poster of the goddess Gayatri, with the corresponding mantra written above her five heads.

with its metaphorical link to the celestial moon, was not an inebriating intoxicant but a life-giving nectar similar to the Greek 'ambrosia'.

The Vedic peoples venerated other planets and their respective deities. Worship of Surya, the sun god, was popular largely through a group of solar deities called the Adityas. Surya was later closely identified with Narayana (Vishnu) and is still venerated indirectly through the chanting of the Gayatri mantra. The famous 13th-century Konorak temple in Orissa testifies to the popularity of sun worship in medieval times. In South India, Surya is still widely adored during the festival of Pongal. Members of the Smarta tradition include Surya as one of their five or six worshipful deities, and his followers, called Sauryas, are sometimes counted among the seven great Hindu traditions.

The worship of planetary deities has endured to the present day. In modern South India, many temples feature an auxiliary shrine, housing nine images set out on a three-by-three grid and called the nava-graha (nine planets). They include the seven planets linked to the weekdays, starting with the sun and moon, plus the two 'shadowy' spheres causing eclipses, namely Rahu and Ketu. It is believed that propitiation of planetary deities can mitigate their channelling of negative karma.

FEMALE DEITIES

Figurines unearthed at Mehrgarh, a key Neolithic archaeological site in modern Pakistan, suggest that goddess worship may be extremely ancient. Such worship was certainly prevalent in the Vedic period. At that time, Prithvi represented the earth, Vak presided over speech, and Usha excelled as the effulgent dawn goddess. These and other female deities generally held subordinate roles, and the Great Goddess – associated with the Supreme – did not emerge until the medieval period. However, like their male counterparts Vishnu and Rudra, many Vedic goddesses survived through assimilation into the later Hindu pantheon. Thus, Pritivi may have evolved into Bhu, one of Vishnu's two consorts; Nirriti, a goddess linked to destruction, may have transformed into the deity now called Kali: and Vak is associated with the modern Sarasvati, perhaps the oldest Hindu goddess.

From about 500BCE onwards, the fire sacrifice was gradually superseded by ritual worship of the sacred image. Attention shifted from the attainment of a temporary heaven to liberation in an eternal world ruled by Vishnu, Shiva or the Goddess. For many Hindus, the continuing presence of many gods and goddesses remains an important sign of the tradition's inclusivity.

Below South Indian women boil sweet rice for the Pongal festival, which primarily honours the sun-god.

THE NORTH CLASSICAL AGE 500BCE–500CE

THE CLOSE OF THE VEDIC PERIOD USHERED IN A GOLDEN, CLASSICAL AGE IN THE NORTH. DURING THIS 1,000-YEAR PERIOD, MANY SECONDARY, SMRITI TEXTS WERE COMPILED.

Above A silver coin, minted around 300BCE, showing the head of the Greek ruler, Seleucus Nicator.

The close of the Vedic age heralded the ascendancy of Hindu culture and the rise of two great powers, the Mauryan and Gupta empires. The period also saw the writing of key scripts, significant changes in the mode of worship and the emergence of three main traditions based on specific focuses of worship.

THE MAURYAN EMPIRE
(c.321–185BCE)

The Magadha kingdom, mentioned in the Mahabharata, had risen to prominence toward the end of the Vedic period. From 350BCE, this eastern kingdom, corresponding to the modern states of Bihar and Bengal, was ruled by the Nanda Dynasty. In 326BCE, Alexander the Great of

Below A map depicting Alexander the Great's route towards India, and his subsequent retreat, which heralded the rise of the Mauryan Empire.

Macedonia alarmed them and other Hindu kings by conquering north-western India and defeating King Porus of the Punjab. However, upon nearing the formidable Magadha kingdom, Alexander's fatigued troops mutinied, turned south toward the coast and eventually moved westward away from the peninsula.

Seizing the opportunity, Chandragupta defeated the Nandas. After ascending the Magadha throne, he repulsed an incursion by remaining Greek forces and established a lasting friendship with their general, Seleucus. This alliance forged cultural ties between Greece and India, which later shared political power over kingdoms centred in Bactria, near the northern border of modern Afghanistan. Chandragupta extended his dominions to establish the mightiest empire of ancient India. His grandson, King Ashoka (r.273–232BCE), further extended

Mauryan territory, but later turned to Buddhism, ushering in an era of peace and non-violence. He propagated Buddhist ideals throughout India and beyond, even as far westward as Mediterranean Greece.

MORAL TEACHINGS

Chandragupta's personal advisor, Chanakya, had previously been a professor at Taxila University. He wrote two important texts: the Artha Shastra, a treatise on statecraft, economic policy and military strategy, and the Niti Shastra, a collection of proverbs still widely read. Many of his teachings were condensations of earlier, oral texts, such as the Manu Smriti (the laws of mankind), which were also committed to writing around this time. The Manu Smriti belongs to a key section of the Vedic canon called the Dharma shastras (moral codes).

The two Hindu epics, the Ramayana and the Mahabharata, were also composed at about this time. They explored the performance of dharma (religious duty), and especially the key roles played by noble kings and their learned advisers, the brahmin priests. By this time, these priests gave less attention to the elaborate Vedic sacrifices and engaged instead in puja, the scheduled worship

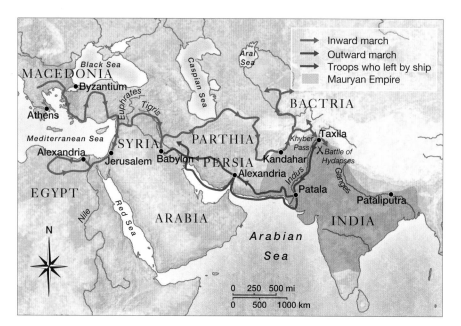

Inward march
Outward march
Troops who left by ship
Mauryan Empire

MACEDONIA
Black Sea
Byzantium
Athens
Mediterranean Sea
Alexandria
SYRIA
Jerusalem
Babylon
EGYPT
Nile
Red Sea
ARABIA
Arabian Sea
Caspian Sea
Aral Sea
Euphrates
Tigris
PARTHIA
PERSIA
Kandahar
Alexandria
BACTRIA
Khyber Pass
Taxila
Battle of Hydaspes
Indus
Patala
Ganges
Pataliputra
INDIA

0   250   500 mi
0   500   1000 km

Left Top of the Ashoka pillar at Sarnath, India, erected by Ashoka. The wheel motif now features on the Indian national flag.

than the Mauryan before it, left a deep cultural impression on India. Historical evidence gleaned from coins, monuments, and travellers' journals indicates the presence of fine cities, well-equipped hospitals, thriving universities and a content and prosperous people.

GUPTA ARTS AND RELIGION

Gupta rule was based on Hindu teachings and divided society into four varnas (classes). Impressive achievements in art, music, literature, philosophy and architecture were also forms of religious expression. The first dances were performed in temples built to facilitate the increasing popularity of ritual worship (puja) and aligned to popular focuses of worship. Three major traditions evolved: two venerating the male deities, Vishnu and Shiva, and a third for the goddess called Shakti. Simultaneously, scholars crystallized the idea of three main deities, the Trimurti, each accompanied by his consort. Brahma, married to Sarasvati, was responsible for creation; Vishnu, married to Lakshmi, became 'the sustainer and protector'; and Shiva, the husband of Shakti, took charge of decay and destruction.

Stories of these deities, written down during this period, now constitute a collection of texts called the 'Puranas'. The most famous describe the activities of Krishna, a form of Vishnu, and the goddess Durga, a warlike form of Shakti. For Shaivas, the Linga Purana, Shiva Purana and Skanda Purana remain core texts glorifying their specific lord.

of sacred images. Simultaneously, the focus of worship had moved from Indra, Agni and other nature gods, to three principal and all-powerful deities: Vishnu (previously a Vedic god), Shiva (earlier called Rudra) and Shakti (the goddess). This period also saw the emergence of renouncer traditions, possibly influenced by Jainism and Buddhism, and also the birth of northern devotional traditions focused on Vasudeva, an alternative name for Krishna, hero of the Mahabharata.

THE GUPTA DYNASTY

The reign of Ashoka was followed by a succession of weaker kings and the gradual erosion of the Mauryan Empire. Powerful nomadic tribes called the Kushans snatched power from the Greeks in Bactria and penetrated India's north-west frontier, extending the influence of Buddhist culture and establishing their eastern capital in Mathura on the Ganges.

The Kushans were expelled by the Gupta dynasty, based in Pataliputra, or present-day Patna in Bihar. For well over two centuries (280–450CE), they ruled all land north of the Vindhya Mountains. The Gupta Empire, though smaller

Right Contemporary classical dancers performing at the Chidambaram temple, Tamil Nadu. Temple construction and dance flourished during the Gupta period.

KINGS AND POETS OF THE SOUTH 500–1200CE

DURING THE NORTHERN CLASSICAL RENAISSANCE, THE TAMIL 'SANGAM' LITERATURE FLOURISHED IN THE SOUTH. AFTER 500CE, THE LONGEST STRIDES IN HINDUISM WERE TAKEN IN THE SOUTH.

The northern Gupta Empire collapsed around 550CE, largely due to military insurgency by the Hunas, the 'White Huns', based in Afghanistan. For a brief span between 535CE and 700CE, the Harsha Empire, centred at Kanauj on the River Ganges, united much of northern India and repulsed the marauding Hunas. King Harsha patronized Buddhism, established diplomatic links with China, and hosted Buddhist pilgrims, including the Chinese historian Hsuan Tsang. Toward the close of Harsha's reign, the Chalukya warrior dynasty assailed his kingdom and, after his death, expanded their empire to embrace central India.

THE CHOLA EMPIRE
(850–1279CE)
With the disintegration of the Harsha Empire around 700CE, and the brief rise of the Chalukyas, power in India shifted southward. The Chola dynasty, which had existed since the 1st century CE, gradually overcame the Chalukyas and other southern dynasties, such as the Pandhyas and Pallavas. At the height of their power, between the 9th and 13th centuries, the Cholas attacked the powerful Pala Dynasty, the Buddhist rulers of Bengal. Their most famous king was Rajaraja, whose great reign was commemorated by the magnificent Shiva temple in Thanjavur.

The Cholas were Shaivas (devotees of Shiva) but supported the other main traditions, Shaktism and Vaishnavism. Particularly in their capital city, Chidambaram, they built many impressive temples featuring *gopurams*, towering gateways decorated with ornate carvings of various gods and goddesses. Shiva remained

Above A 12th-century bronze of Lord Shiva as Nataraja, the 'king of dancers' revered by the southern Chola emperors.

the most popular deity, particularly in his form as Nataraja, the 'king of dancers'. The Cholas were perhaps the first Indian rulers to maintain a fleet to extend their territory beyond the peninsula.

SOUTH-EAST ASIA
Through trade and commerce, Hinduism may have reached Indo-China and Indonesia as early as the 1st century CE. Aided by their navy,

Below Map showing the extent of Chola influence in South-east Asia. The huge temples at Angkor Wat in modern Cambodia were built at the height of Chola power.

Below An 11th-century Shiva temple in Cholapuram, capital of the Chola dynasty.

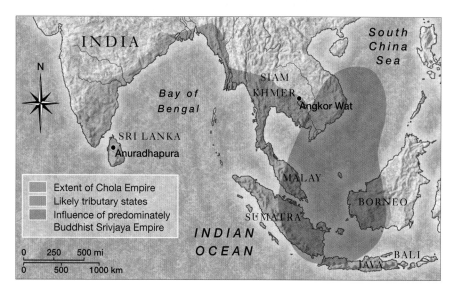

Above Traditional painting of Andal, the only woman among the 12 devotional saints called 'Alvars'.

the Chola Empire further colonized countries to the south and south-east, including the Maldive Islands, Sri Lanka and lands belonging to the largely Buddhist Srivijaya Empire in Indonesia, including Malaya, Java and Sumatra. On the Indo-China peninsula, Chola armies exacted tribute from the rulers of Siam (present-day Thailand) and the Khmer kingdom (modern-day Cambodia).

Around this time, Hinduism reached the island of Bali, where it remains the principal religion. Throughout South-east Asia, Hindu beliefs and practices intertwined with Buddhist and native traditions. This mixed culture still exists in many parts of Indo-China and Indonesia, as evident in the contin-uing use of long Sanskrit names and the cultural popularity of the Mahabharata and the Ramayana.

SOUTHERN POET-SAINTS

Between the 6th and 10th centuries CE, poet-saints in southern India helped Hinduism move away from the strict, brahmin-controlled ritual of the Vedic times. Focus on a personal God, rather than an impersonal absolute, laid early foundations for

modern Hinduism. Writing in the Tamil tongue, the poet-saints established its importance as a sacred language, much like Sanskrit in the north.

Among the poet-saints were the 63 Nayanmars, fervent devotees of Shiva. Largely unconcerned with scholarship, they immersed them-selves in practical service, such as cleaning temple premises, lighting the lamps, stringing flower garlands, feeding the devotees and perform-ing other menial tasks. They regarded worship of Lord Shiva's devotees to be paramount, even higher than the worship of God himself. The Nayanmars helped establish the important tradition now called Shaiva Siddhanta.

The Vaishnava (Vishnu-worship-ping) equivalents of the Nayanmars were the 12 Alvars, including the celebrated female saint, Andal. The 9th-century scholar, Nathamuni, compiled the poems of the 12 Alvars into an anthology of 4,000 verses called the 'Divya Prabhandham'. Singing the praises of Vishnu in his form as the four-handed Narayana it remains a core text, recited daily, in the famous Shrirangam Temple. Nathamuni also initiated the impor-tant tradition called Shri Vaishnavism.

BHAKTI MOVEMENTS

The poet-saints came from all occu-pations and cared little for the Hindu social structure, which by then had become rigid and hereditary. By accepting disciples from all social classes, the saints challenged the authority of caste-conscious brah-mins. The poet-saints gave rise to popular bhakti (devotional) move-ments that later swept north to embrace all of India. One of the first was founded in the 12th century by a scholar called Basavanna. Members were called Lingayats, named for always carrying a miniature lingam, the cylindrical black stone represent-ing Lord Shiva. The Lingayats believed in one God and rejected the Vedas, considering them to be polytheistic. They championed the underdog, teaching about the equal-ity of all beings and, unusually for the time, accepting women as gurus (religious teachers). However, this upsurge of devotion was more than mere sentiment, and was accompa-nied by seminal developments in scholarship and the foundation of key doctrinal lineages.

Below Hindu temples on the Indonesian island of Bali, colonized by the Cholas.

Who Founded Hinduism?

HINDUISM FEATURES NO SINGLE FOUNDER. INSTEAD, SEVERAL KEY FIGURES STARTED THIER OWN SPECIFIC TRADITIONS AND SACRED LINEAGES, AND TAUGHT DISTINCTIVE BRANCHES OF PHILOSOPHY.

Almost universally, God is considered the ultimate source of religion, and many sacred lineages (*sampradayas*) still consider their founder to be an avatara, a descent of God. The broad denominations are defined by their chosen deity, and sub-groups usually by their following a specific saint or scholar.

THE ANCIENT RISHIS

Tradition holds that in ancient times there lived seven great rishis, sages and seers who transmitted the universal wisdom later recorded in Vedic texts. The rishis, born from the mind of the creator Brahma, are often associated with the seven stars of the Plough. Hindu families claim to trace their dynasty (gotra) to one of the seven, whose names include Atri, Bhrigu, Angira, Gautama, Vashishta, Bharadvaja and Vishvamitra (though there are variant lists). These names appear repeatedly in the stories of the Epics, Puranas, and other texts. Although the rishis were born shortly after creation, some are reputed to be still alive. More recent rishis include the founders of the Six Darshanas (philosophical schools), most notably Vyasa who inaugurated Vedanta philosophy.

SHANKARA

After the fall of the northern Gupta dynasty, and while the poet-saints expounded devotion in the

Above The Plough contains the seven brightest stars in the constellation Ursa Major. They are often associated with the seven sages and seers known as the rishis.

Tamil-speaking south, key thinkers (acharyas) started laying foundations for modern Hindu thought. Each acharya founded a branch of theology, transmitted through a specific sampradaya, a lineage of teachers and students. These founding acharyas reinforced the importance of the guru-disciple relationship.

The first prominent acharya was Shankara, also called Shankaracharya (780–812CE). Born in today's southern state of Kerala, he was instructed by his guru, Govinda Bhagavatapada – disciple of the renowned author Gaudapada – to write commentaries on Vedanta philosophy. By Shankara's time, Hinduism had lost momentum due to the competing influence of the non-Vedic religions, Jainism and Buddhism. By travelling throughout India and defeating contesting scholars, Shankara re-established the authority of the Vedic literature. He founded the Advaita school of Vedanta by equating the individual self with God. He also augmented the three main denominations – Vaishnavism, Shaivism and Shaktism – by revitalizing and formalizing a fourth, the Smarta tradition.

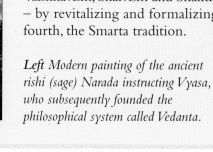

Left Modern painting of the ancient rishi (sage) Narada instructing Vyasa, who subsequently founded the philosophical system called Vedanta.

EARLY SHAIVA FOUNDERS

Some consider Shankara an incarnation of Lord Shiva, who is thought to have previously descended as Lakulisha (*c.*200CE). Considered the founder of Shaivism, or at least its first formal guru, Lakulisha is credited with compiling the Pashupati Sutra texts, central to the oldest Shaiva sect, the Pashupatis. The other five main Shaiva groups have their own founders.

One of the greatest was Vasugupta (*c.*860–925CE) who revealed the Shiva Sutras and founded the system called Kashmir Shaivism. Its greatest scholar was Abhinavagupta (*c.*950CE) who, unlike Shankara, favoured non-Vedic texts called Tantras. Of his 35 works, the largest is Tantraloka, an extensive treatise central to modern Kashmiri Shaivism and to many Shakti traditions. Since Abhinavagupta's time, there have been several other great Shaiva scholars, including Gorakshanatha (the Natha tradition), Basavanna (the Lingayats) and Rishi Tirumular

Below Madhva (1238–1317), depicted here with previous incarnations, lived after two other key scholars of Vedanta, namely Shankara and Ramanuja.

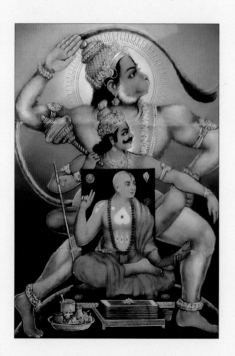

Above Rocky Island, Kanyakumari, is an important pilgrimage site for the followers of Swami Vivekananda.

(Shaiva Siddhanta). Srikantha is notable for founding a branch of Vedanta and the corresponding Shaiva Advaita School.

RAMANUJA AND MADHVA

The four main Vaishnava lineages also subscribe to Vedanta. Ramanuja (1017–1137) is the acharya for the south-Indian Shri Vaishnava sampradaya, founded by Nathamuni (*c.*824–900CE). Ramanuja qualified Shankara's doctrine by proposing that God is not only the formless, but also a person with spiritual form. Ramanuja's theology of 'qualified monism' laid solid foundations for other monotheistic doctrines contesting Shankara's monism.

More strongly than Ramanuja before him, Madhva (1238–1317) stressed the personal form of God (as Krishna) and his eternal distinction from the soul. Madhva's philosophy, called 'pure dualism', is unique in Hinduism in advocating an eternal hell for sinners. The headquarters of the Madhva tradition are in Udupi in Karnataka.

The acharyas for the two other Vaishnava lineages are Nimbarka, whose dates are uncertain, and Vallabha (1481–1543), who followed the footsteps of Vishnuswami (dates unknown). Vallabha started the Pushti Marg ('path of nourishment') still popular in Gujarat and Rajasthan.

LATER FOUNDERS

After the main acharyas, many others founded subsequent groups, often as branches of previous lineages. The Ramakrishna Mission, founded by Vivekananda, pursued Shankara's Advaita doctrine. The Swaminarayan Movement, founded by Sahajananda Swami (1781–1830), modified and extended Ramanuja's teachings.

During that period of British rule in India, Hindu intellectuals founded more radical 'reform movements', attempting either to break from tradition or to revert to fundamental Vedic teachings. These movements still complement the main traditional lineages. Although some contemporary gurus derive authority solely from personal charisma, many still claim descent from previous founders and acharyas. The modern Hare Krishna movement, founded by Bhaktivedanta Swami, declares unbroken links to Madhva but also draws heavily on Ramanuja's thought.

ISLAM GAINS GROUND IN INDIA 1192–1526CE

WHILST HINDU KINGDOMS PROSPERED IN THE SOUTH, RELIGIOUS LIFE IN THE NORTH WAS THREATENED, SPECIFICALLY BY THE ARRIVAL OF A RADICALLY DIFFERENT RELIGION AND CULTURE.

In the 7th century CE, the new religion of Islam had reached Indian shores via merchants plying the Arabian Sea. A hundred years later, Iraqi Arabs invaded and occupied the north-western state of Sind. Thereafter, Muslim warlords from Turkey and Central Asia superseded Persia as the major power to India's west, and began raiding through her vulnerable north-west frontier.

EARLY RAIDS

Particularly brutal were the incursions of Mahmud of Ghazni (971–1030), the Afghan emperor. As a zealous Sunni Muslim, he plundered the northern states 17 times, sacking Hindu temples and plundering their considerable wealth. In 1025, he razed the Shiva temple in Somnatha, slaughtered its residents and enchained thousands of slaves. Legend holds that, after personally hacking the sacred image to pieces, he sent the fragments back to Gazni for setting in the steps of a new mosque. Mahmud annexed much of north-western India, including modern Pakistan and Indian Punjab. However, his death in 1030 heralded the gradual erosion of his vast empire. Hindu kings reclaimed Punjab and, to the west of Gazni, Turks and Afghans from the city of Ghor seized power and continued the assault on northern India.

THE DELHI SULTANATE

To repulse these attacks, King Prithviraj consolidated the military might of the Rajputs, warriors

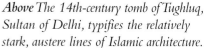

Above The 14th-century tomb of Tughluq, Sultan of Delhi, typifies the relatively stark, austere lines of Islamic architecture.

claiming ancestry from the glorious days of Lord Rama. However, in 1192, Muhammad of Ghor defeated Prithviraj at the second battle of Tarain and triumphantly entered Delhi. After Muhammad's assassination in 1206, Qutb ud-Din established the first Muslim kingdom in India.

The Delhi Sultanate refers to the Muslim dynasties and sultans who, from 1206 to 1526, subdued the entire sub-continent, with the exception

Left The 13th-century sun temple in Konark, Orissa, shows the fluid, sensual nature of Hindu architecture at that time.

THE BIRTH OF SIKHISM

Guru Nanak (1469–1539), the founder of the Sikh religion, was influenced by the mystical northern *sant* (saint) tradition. He taught the practice of chanting God's holy names, the equality of all people and the importance of *seva*, service to others. Nanak's new faith was at first closely connected to Hinduism, though conspicuous by its military flavour in first resisting the Mughals and later the British. Only much later on did Sikhism define itself as a religion quite distinct from Hinduism.

Right The saint Kabir, a lowly weaver, opposed social and religious discrimination. He drew inspiration from Sufism and the northern Sant tradition, which both favoured an impersonal Supreme.

of Kashmir in the far north and the southern Hindu kingdom of Vijayanagara. The fall of Delhi in 1192 heralded over five centuries of Muslim rule, which left a deep and enduring impression on India's religious landscape.

AREAS OF CONFLICT

Islam and Hinduism bore conflicting codes of social behaviour. Islam was inflexible, authoritarian and obligatory, and it stressed the equality of all within its community of 'believers'. Hinduism was flexible, discriminating and hierarchical, and it celebrated internal diversity. Religious beliefs were also different. Islam was austerely monotheistic, whereas Hinduism seemed richly polytheistic, though underpinned by inclusive forms of monotheism. For Muslims, image worship was an abomination; for Hindus it was an expression of divine love. For Muslims, the cow was a valuable source of meat; for Hindus, she was a gentle and revered mother who provided milk.

DEVOTIONAL POEMS

The bhakti saints opposed both caste practices and rigidly sectarian religion. They recognized the commonality of God, as sardonically expressed by Kabir:

'Rama, Rama!', chants the Hindu,
'Allah is one', proclaims the Muslim,
But my Lord pervades all.
The God of Hindus lives in
  the temple.
The God of Muslims resides in
  the mosque.
Who resides where there are
Neither temples nor mosques?

However, by the time Muslims arrived, Hinduism had developed its own brand of discrimination. The ancient Indian system of four varnas had become strictly hereditary. Birth in a high family ensured a prestigious livelihood. Those born in lower varnas, even if professionally talented, were condemned to poorly paid menial work. Many low-caste Hindus were either excluded from religious life or over-dependent on brahmins eager to monopolize their prestigious positions. Muslim rule exacerbated this marginalization by creating a governing elite, reinforcing class differences and largely excluding Hindus from civic life.

DEVOTION SWEEPS NORTH

From 1200 CE onward, religious leaders arose from among the people, teaching personal piety and spiritual egalitarianism. The northern Sant (saint) tradition, which included Kabir, was highly eclectic, fusing

Hindu devotion with Sufism and ascetic yoga. Many bhakti traditions, such as the Ramanandi ascetic lineage, adopted forms of Vedanta philosophy and extended the teachings of Ramanuja and Madhva. Travelling saints also composed their own songs, poems and prayers, in local languages rather than Sanskrit, and popularized the glorification of God, ecstatic dancing, and the musical recitation of mantras.

Right The Vakari tradition of Maharashtra, shown here in procession, comes from the northern Sant tradition and from bhakti saints like Namdev, who preceded Kabir.

THE MUGHAL EMPIRE 1526–1858

THE DELHI SULTANATE GAVE WAY TO THE GREAT MUGHAL DYNASTY. THIS PERIOD SAW BOTH SOCIO-RELIGIOUS DISCORD AND SPIRITED ATTEMPTS TO TRANSCEND SOCIAL AND RELIGIOUS DIVISIONS.

Due to fierce rivalry between different factions, the Delhi Sultanate gradually descended into civil war. In 1398, Delhi was destroyed by Timur, a warlord claiming descent from the Mongol emperor, Genghis Khan. The Sultanate never fully recovered, and, in 1526, the capital eventually fell to Babur, a Muslim emperor from Central Asia. Babur established the Mughal dynasty, which ruled much of India for the next three centuries. His son, Humayun, spent much of his reign in exile and died during his resurgence and the consolidation of Mughal power.

AKBAR THE GREAT
The Mughal Empire reached the peak of its glory, though not its greatest territorial size, under Humayan's son, Akbar. Born and raised in India, Akbar displayed a tolerant attitude toward all religions, celebrating Hindu festivals such as Divali and inviting to religious debates not only Muslims, but also Hindus, Sikhs and Christians. He also encouraged members of other religions to enter his court, and founded a new philosophy called Din Ilahi which advocates the equality of all faith systems. During his long reign (1542–1605), Akbar extended the kingdom and left many fine buildings and works of art. He is remembered as the greatest of the Mughal emperors.

AURANGZEB
Akbar was succeeded by his son and then by his grandson, Shah Jahan (1592–1666), famed for building the Taj Mahal (in Agra) and the Red Fort (in Delhi). Shah Jahan's son, Aurangzeb, was tyrannical, slaying his brothers, imprisoning his father and proclaiming himself emperor. During his long reign (1668–1707), he discriminated against Hindus, imposing special taxes on them and defacing their temples and sacred images.

Aurangzeb's religious policies contributed to Muslim-Hindu conflict in India, creating resentment that endures to modern times. Where Aurangzeb did excel was in expanding Mughal territory, especially in the south. Upon his death, the Mughal Empire was at its largest, but rapidly fell into an irrecoverable

Above Painted c.1590, this miniature depicts the court of Emperor Akbar, who welcomed scholars from many religions.

decline. Later emperors witnessed the rise of British power, and concluded with Bahadur Shah II, the last Mughal emperor, who was exiled to Burma and died in 1857.

NEW HINDU KINGDOMS
During Muslim rule, two new Hindu kingdoms arose. In the south, the fabulously wealthy Vijayanagar (City of Victory) resisted the military might of both the Delhi Sultanate and the Mughals until its final collapse in 1565. This marked the end of the south as an autonomous political area. However, a more formidable foe of the Mughals emerged on the west coast of India, in the mountainous Maratha kingdom. The Maratha king Shivaji (1630–1680) and his successors relentlessly harassed Aurangzeb, hastening the end of Mughal dominion. Shivaji was a resistance fighter who exemplified the ancient Hindu ideal of a stern yet chivalrous warrior. For many modern Hindus, he remains a symbol of the righteous struggle against intolerance and oppression.

Left A modern statue of the 17th-century warrior king, Shivaji, who harassed the forces of Aurangzeb and the declining Mughal Empire.

Above A plaster statue of Mirabai, a popular medieval bhakti saint.

HINDUISM UNDER THE MUGHALS

Under much Muslim rule, Hindus were required to pay the discriminatory jizya tax, inclining many, especially the poor, to convert to Islam. Some people were forcibly converted through intimidation or violence. By the end of the period of Mughal rule, almost a quarter of the Hindu population had embraced Islam, mainly in the north-western and eastern provinces.

At the same time, the bhakti movement were intent on developing personal devotion irrespective of social and political circumstance. The 'bhakti saints' drew on the earlier devotional sentiments of the southern poet-saints, but rather than worshipping Shiva and Vishnu, they focused more on Rama and Krishna, two of the principal incarnations of Vishnu.

The female poet Mirabai was apparently visited by Akbar who, disguised as a mendicant, was so moved by her singing that he draped her Krishna image with a diamond necklace. Mirabai is reported to have met the great scholar and renunciant Jiva Goswami (c.1515–1618), who wrote key theological texts for the Bengali Vaishnava movement started by the charismatic saint Chaitanya (1486–1534). At the same time, Vallabha's Pushti Marg, 'the past of nourishment', later popular in

Below An 18th-century, Mughal-style painting of Radha and Krishna, deities adored by many devotional movements.

Rajasthan and Gujarat, had just started. Legend holds that Vallabha was born as his parents fled Muslim atrocities in Varanasi prior to Mughal rule. In the West Indian state of Maharashtra, Tukaram (1606–50) appeared in the long 'Varkari' tradition, which worshipped Krishna, and is reputed to have instructed Shivaji, the great resistance fighter.

A PERSONAL GOD

Unlike Kabir, many later bhakti saints propounded the notion of a personal God. Some criticized the doctrine of absolute monism, as Tukaram does in this poem.

This is why I abandoned home
    for the forest;
My love would be spoiled by
    the evil eye.
By listening to this doctrine
    of unity
I will lose my love for the Lord.
Tuka declares, 'This idea is false,
The notion that "God and I
    are one".
I will not let it divert me from
    his sacred service.'

THE USE OF THE TERM HINDUISM

With the arrival of Islam, the ancient and inclusive tradition of Sanatana Dharma (as Hindus often call it) was forced to redefine itself. The ancient Persians had first coined the term 'Hindu' around the 8th century, referring to the people living on the far side of the River Indus. By the 1400s, the term had been adopted by practitioners, to distinguish themselves from members of other religions. Despite this, only later, during British domination of India, was the term 'Hinduism' first used.

BRITISH RULE AND HINDU REFORM 1757–1947

THE MUSLIM DOMINATION OF INDIA SAW THE EMERGENCE OF EGALITARIAN, DEVOTIONAL TRADITIONS. BRITISH RULE PROMOTED A MORE POLITICALLY AWARE RESPONSE TO ALIEN FAITH AND CULTURE.

In 1498, Vasco da Gama from Portugal became the first European to land in India, at the western port of Calicut. Subsequently, in 1510, the Portuguese ruthlessly conquered Goa. The wealth of India, especially her spices and textiles, also attracted the attention of many Dutch, French and British explorers. In 1610 the British East India Company established a trading post in Surat and, within eight decades, further bases in Madras, Bombay and Calcutta. The company forged trade agreements with Mughal rulers and recruited local men into their private armies. As the East India Company expanded, tensions with local rulers led to armed conflict. Robert Clive's decisive victory at the Battle of Plassey (1757), in Bengal, heralded

Above Lord Robert Clive (1725–74), twice governor of Bengal, painted around 1764 by Thomas Gainsborough.

the end of the Mughal Empire. Within 12 years the East India Company had crushed its competitors, practically monopolizing European trade in India.

However, discontent at the expanding foreign presence was rife. In 1857, rumour spread among Indian troops that their rifle bullets were greased with the lard of cows and pigs, inconsistent with both Hindu and Muslim beliefs. The army rebelled during the Indian Mutiny, which many Hindus now call 'The First War of Independence'. The ensuing bloodshed prompted the British government to take direct control of India in 1857 and, 20 years later, Queen Victoria received the accolade, 'Empress of India'.

THE REFORM MOVEMENTS

The early colonialists gave Hindus free rein in their religious practice. Later, zealous missionaries, scholars and government officials deliberately attempted to convert Hindus to Christianity, and to 'civilize' them. Convinced of the moral supremacy of Christianity, Thomas Macaulay deliberately set about creating 'a class

Below Depiction of the capture of two Indian guns in 1858, during what the British termed 'the Indian Mutiny'.

The Indian Mutiny was sparked by apathy toward Hindu and Muslim belief. Hindu recruits objected that their bullets were greased with the lard of slaughtered cattle. For Hindus, the milk-providing cow was considered a mother-figure. The bull, extensively used in ploughing, was considered a father figure, the 'bread-winner' and an emblem of Dharma (religion). For these reasons, coupled with the ideal of ahimsa (non-violence), the cow and bull are still offered special respect. As many Hindus are vegetarian, milk products are considered essential for a balanced diet. Ghee (clarified butter) is used extensively: in cooking, for temple lamps and during such rituals as the ancient fire sacrifice.

The English idiom 'sacred cow' evolved in India to refer to irrational or superstitious belief. This derogatory term may reflect broad differences between Western and Hindu worldviews. Hindu scholarship widely

THE SACRED COW

Above Go-puja, veneration of the cow, during temple festivities in the sacred town of Vrindavana, north India.

accepts, without undue apprehension, the existence of paranormal phenomena. For example, human perception of ghosts is largely explained through reincarnation, by which the subtle body carries the soul to its next destination. Astrology is a science practised by respectable brahmins,

using Jyotisha, one of the six subsidiary Vedic texts. Mystical powers are widely accepted as credible, and not especially miraculous.

Some reform movements objected to what they also deemed superstition. To resist them, orthodox traditions collectively called themselves 'sanatanist', drawing on ideas of the Sanatana Dharma (eternal religion). These traditionalists argued that it is logical to accept life's spiritual dimensions, beyond direct perception. They considered the systematic abuse of cattle to be irrational and morally reprehensible. Just as colonial scholars constructed biased stereotypes of Hindus, so Hindus formed caricatures of Westerners; as unhygienic meat-eaters with a theology that propounded just one life and inadequately addressed the problem of evil and suffering. For many Hindus, cow slaughter begets human misfortune and remains a sign of incivility.

---

of persons Indian in blood and colour, but English in taste, in opinions, in morals and in intellect'. English became the official language for education. These policies, and the growing contact between Hinduism and the West, spawned various Hindu 'reform movements'. While they attempted to resist or influence change, they also assimilated many Christian and Western ideas.

One of the most influential groups was the Brahmo Sabha, founded in 1828 by Ram Mohan Roy and later renamed the Brahmo Samaj. Impressed by Christian theology, Ram Mohan Roy disagreed with caste practice, image worship and the idea of reincarnation. The

Right Portrait of Ram Mohan Roy (1774–1833), founder of one of the most influential 'reform movements'.

Arya Samaj, founded in 1875 by Swami Dayananda, took a different line. It wished to halt the Christian onslaught and return to the ancient, Vedic religion, purging its tradition of later Puranic impositions: pilgrimage, ritual bathing and veneration of sacred images. Its main form of worship remains the ancient, Vedic fire ceremony.

These reform movements had relatively little effect on popular Hindu practice, and the core traditions continued to predominate. However, reformers succeeded in making Hindus more reflective and aware of their own identity as a separate religion. They also spawned nationalist movements, which tried to rid India of foreign rule. British economic policy also resulted in the emigration of Hindus to other parts of the Empire.

MIGRATION TO THE COLONIES 1834–c.1900

BRITISH RULE IN INDIA HAD A HUGE IMPACT NOT ONLY ON HINDU THOUGHT, BUT ON MIGRATION AND THE SUBSEQUENT ESTABLISHMENT OF HINDU COMMUNITIES THROUGHOUT THE WORLD.

Emigration from India had been prevalent since the first millennium CE, mainly to South-east Asia for commercial reasons. However, during the colonial period, emigration occurred on an unprecedented scale, largely to provide inexpensive labour to the Dutch, French and British colonies. During the 19th century, the number of emigrants from India exceeded one-and-a-half million.

THE CARIBBEAN
In the British Caribbean, the abolition and phasing out of slavery, from 1834 onward, precipitated a manpower crisis. Western workers were hardly interested, largely due to the unhealthy and perilous tropical climate. Seeking alternative sources of cheap labour, the colonial governments turned their attention to densely populated India.

Below Map showing global Hindu migration from around 1840 until the early 1900s.

Beginning in the 1840s, indentured labourers, workers bound by contract, underwent the long and hazardous voyage to the Caribbean. For consenting to work for a specified number of years, they were promised fair wages and return tickets. However, due to prolonged debt, dishonest contracts and aspirations to build a new life, few returned home. The first Indians to arrive, mainly from Hindi-speaking north India, worked as labourers for the sugar industry in Trinidad. Others sailed to French Guyana and the Dutch island of Surinam to work on sugar and rubber plantations.

SOUTH-EAST ASIA AND AFRICA
In 1870 the British took formal control of the western states of Malay. Many Tamils, from what is now the southern state of Tamil Nadu, were subsequently shipped there to toil in the tin mines, railways, and rubber plantations. Others emigrated to Singapore and Burma

Above Indentured workers at a British tea plantation in Sri Lanka (formerly Ceylon) around 1900.

(present-day Myanmar). From 1879, thousands sailed east to the Fiji islands to labour on the sugar and cotton estates. Indians, many of them Hindus, also arrived on the Island of Mauritius, off the east coast of Africa, and on the adjacent French island of Reunion. Many Gujarati merchants and builders emigrated to East Africa, and other Indians to South

MIGRATION AND HINDU CULTURE
Emigration affected Hindu practice. As workers aspired for acceptance by their host communities, they often assimilated local lifestyle norms. The men, especially, began to wear Western clothes. They modified their eating habits, abandoning traditional, often vegetarian, diets. However, in some instances, Hindus living outside India became stricter, aware of the need to preserve their heritage, and bequeath it to their children and grandchildren. Emigration highlighted the struggle to maintain tradition, while at the same time adjusting appropriately to new situations.

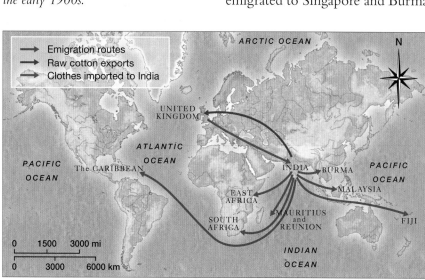

Emigration routes
Raw cotton exports
Clothes imported to India

ARCTIC OCEAN

N

UNITED KINGDOM

ATLANTIC OCEAN

PACIFIC OCEAN

The CARIBBEAN

INDIA   BURMA   PACIFIC OCEAN

EAST AFRICA   MALAYSIA

SOUTH AFRICA   MAURITIUS and REUNION   FIJI

INDIAN OCEAN

0   1500   3000 mi
0   3000   6000 km

Africa, to lay railways or mine gold. It was in South Africa that Mohandas K. Gandhi, the most famous modern Hindu, practised law. He was alarmed at colonial abuse and, through personal experience, at the brutal treatment of Africans and Indians as second-class citizens.

THE COTTON TRADE

Shortly after his return to India in 1915, Gandhi stepped on to the political stage. He objected to the British economic policy of cultivating cash crops, such as indigo, despite a devastating famine. He also protested against the export of raw Indian cotton to Manchester and the subsequent import of clothes at inflated prices. His struggle for fair trade, and the preservation of India's village-based economy, became part of a burgeoning movement seeking to abolish colonial exploitation.

Frustration with British rule, and the influence of the intellectual reform movements, spawned various nationalist organizations. In 1909, leading members of the Arya Samaj founded the Hindu Mahasabha, 'the Great Hindu Assembly', to give Hindus a political voice. The Mahasabha declared India to be

Below The Triveni temple, built in Trinidad in 2002, testifies to the long-term influence of Hindu migration.

Hindustan, 'the land of the Hindus' and demanded government according to Hindu law. In 1932, their leader, Vir Savarkar, coined the term Hindutva. It literally means 'Hinduness', but the term is largely associated with organizations that promote Hindu nationalism. These movements included the Rashtriya Swayamsevak Sangh (RSS), established in 1925 to protect 'the interests of the people who treat India as their motherland'.

Gandhi led by example. Intent on undermining the British textile industry, his followers boycotted cloth milled in Western factories, and

Above Gandhi greeted jubilantly at the Greenfield Mill at Darwen, Lancashire, in 1931. He was trying to resolve trade tensions exacerbated by his boycott of milled cloth.

wore only home-spun cotton called 'khadi'. In 1939, he organized a 384-kilometre (238-mile) march to the sea, where demonstrators illegally manufactured their own salt, protesting against the British salt tax. In all these protests, Gandhi insisted on non-violence and 'passive resistance', even in responding to aggression. He also addressed mounting social ills, and upheld the rights of the socially excluded untouchables, whom he called 'harijans' (the children of God). However, Gandhi the reformer was in many ways a traditionalist, drawing strength and conviction from Hindu teachings, especially as found in the Ramayana and the Bhagavad-gita. Although he fought against the hereditary caste system, he believed in the original system of four varnas. He prayed daily, ate simple vegetarian food, and undertook long fasts as a means of both self-purification and social protest. In 1942, he started the 'Quit India' movement.

INDIAN PARTITION AND INDEPENDENCE 1947–

INDIAN INDEPENDENCE PROMISED NEW OPPORTUNITIES. IT ALSO SOWED THE SEEDS OF RELIGIOUS STRIFE, EXACERBATING TENSIONS BETWEEN HINDUISM AS A SPIRITUAL PATH AND AS A POLITICAL VEHICLE.

Gandhi led the initial negotiations for independence, which continued in earnest after the close of World War II (1939–45). Moves towards self-governance fuelled tensions between Hindus and Muslims. For the minority Islamic community, the imminent Hindu government promised no improvement on British rule. Gandhi pleaded for unity between the two groups. However, in 1946, Muhammed Jinnah, head of the Muslim League, conveyed the message that for his community an

Below Pandit Jawaharlal Nehru (1889–1964) conversing with Indian Independence leader Mahatma Gandhi in Bombay, 1946.

undivided India was no longer possible. Muslims were not prepared to live under a Hindu government.

PARTITION

On 15 August 1947, Indian independence coincided with the birth of a new nation, Pakistan. It consisted of two separate, predominantly Muslim states carved from the north-western and eastern parts of former Indian territory. Partition was marred by unprecedented horrors. Around half a million people perished as more than 11 million refugees – Hindus, Muslims, and Sikhs – criss-crossed the newly drawn borders. The following year, Gandhi, distraught by partition and the ensuing genocide, was

Above The corpse of a Calcutta resident killed in 1946 during communal riots between Hindus and Muslims.

assassinated, gunned down by a Hindu fanatic. His former ally, Jawaharlal Nehru, was sworn in as India's first prime minister.

BANGLADESH

East and West Pakistan constituted a single country divided by a thousand miles of Indian land, and by a gulf of cultural and linguistic differences. Feeling neglected by their government in West Pakistan, the eastern state declared independence in 1971, calling itself 'Bangladesh'. News reports exposed further mass slaughter, particularly of Bangladeshi students and intellectuals. In the ensuing war of independence, Bangladesh emerged victorious and the international community formally recognized her sovereignty in 1979. Her boundaries still embrace many Hindu pilgrimage sites, especially those connected to Bengali Vaishnavism.

KASHMIR

After partition, India forcibly assimilated smaller territories, including the independent Hyderabad, French India and later, in 1961, Portuguese Goa. Kashmir, a largely autonomous state, chose to join India, despite its Muslim majority. Pakistan objected, culminating in the

first Indo-Pakistan War (1948). A stalemate gave way to a ceasefire, and finally to the assimilation of Kashmir into India. Some boundaries remained unclear, and religious tensions continued into the 21st century, marring the prospects for a region once famed for its scenic landscapes and rich religious heritage. The cave at Amarnath, which is dedicated to Lord Shiva, remains an important Hindu pilgrimage site.

NEPAL

Although India and Pakistan divided on religious lines, the new secular India was neutral in matters of religion. After partition, the only remaining Hindu country in the world was Nepal, lying between India and China. It also became secular after the fall of the monarchy in 2008, with approximately three-quarters of its population still Hindus. Many Hindus of Nepalese origin also live in the Himalayan kingdom of Bhutan, and comprise a quarter of its population.

Right India after partition, showing countries and areas of specific contention. More recently, ideas of 'sacred land' have been used to promote Hindu nationalism.

Below A Hindu temple in a valley within the disputed territory of Kashmir.

INDIA AS A SACRED LAND

The relationship between Hinduism and India is contentious. The terms 'India' and 'Indian' are variously used, referring to the geographical land mass, the people living there, or the nation state. As a geographical area, India's natural features are associated with thousands of saints and avataras, and pilgrims often throng to its holy sites, walking barefoot out of respect for sacred ground. There has also developed a widespread belief that crossing the ocean rendered a Hindu impure, possibly because maintaining a vegetarian diet would be difficult. Some, mirroring the hereditary caste-system, suggest that a Hindu is identified exclusively by birth in a Hindu family.

Hindu ideas of sanctity don't generally derive from thinking their own religion 'special' (and thus sacred) but from the palpable presence of the divine in specific spots. Some Hindu texts condemn nationalism as a sign of misidentification

with the external body. Such medieval bhakti saints as Kabir and Chaitanya also criticized any sectarian or nationalistic attitude, despite Indian occupation by Muslim rulers.

However, India's domination by foreign powers highlighted issues of protecting sacred land from aggressors, and from adversarial, proselytizing religions. The notion of sacred land has also been used for political purposes. Some have argued that Hinduism is an Indian religion, and that India should be a Hindu nation. Other Hindus claim the Indian peninsula to be special simply for its being conducive to spiritual development. For them, the strength and durability of Hinduism lies in its inclusivity, and its celebration of diversity. Overall, the precise relationship between India and Hinduism remains debatable, especially since increasing numbers of Hindus are born abroad, or come from non-Indian families.

A GLOBAL HINDUISM

INDIAN INDEPENDENCE MARKED THE IMMINENT DISSOLUTION OF THE BRITISH EMPIRE. IN PURSUIT OF INDIA'S EXAMPLE, MANY OTHER COLONIES SOUGHT INDEPENDENCE, ESPECIALLY IN THE 1960s.

In rapid succession, the East African colonies achieved self-rule: Uganda in 1962, Kenya in 1963 and the newly created Tanzania in 1964. Through policies known as 'Africanization', wealth and position were returned to Africans.

LEAVING EAST AFRICA

Many Indians opted to leave or were forcibly expelled, often relinquishing considerable wealth and business assets. As British citizens, many opted to settle within the United Kingdom, as factory workers or as self-employed grocers, newsagents and clothing manufacturers. Others filled emerging vacancies in the National Health Service. The first austere temples, often housed in disused school or church buildings, also served as community centres, and worship was highly eclectic, embracing many traditions and focuses. Although initially disadvantaged, the British Hindu community gradually integrated and

Below Map of Hindu migration patterns in the latter half of the 20th century following Indian independence.

established itself, and by the year 2000 had excelled in educational and professional fields. The many magnificent purpose-built temples, replacing the converted halls, testified to the growing wealth, prestige and influence of the Hindu community.

MIGRATION FROM INDIA

During the second half of the 20th century, many Hindus emigrated directly from India. Particularly popular was North America, especially the USA, where by 2000 the community numbered almost 1.5 million. Unlike their British counterparts, many were well-placed professionals, such as engineers and IT specialists. Other Indians moved to Europe, often from southern India and Sri Lanka, establishing the presence of the previously under-represented southern Hindu traditions. Since 1965, many Hindus have sought economic advantage in the oil-rich Arab States around the Persian Gulf. About one million now live there, mainly in Bahrain, Kuwait, Yemen, Saudi Arabia and the United Arab Emirates. They often support

Above A British mandir dedicated to the goddess Shakti. Hindu migrants from Africa established it around 1970 in a disused church hall.

relatives in India, where the money sent home is worth far more due to the comparatively low cost of living.

WORLDWIDE MOVEMENTS

During the post-independence era, many gurus travelled west to offer spiritual support to the fledgling communities in Europe and America. At the same time, westerners themselves were increasingly enamoured by Indian thought and culture, especially during the hippie movement of the 1960s, with its tendency to question and relinquish a materialistic way of life. Although the number of Western Hindus remained relatively small, practices such as yoga and meditation were gradually assimilated into society, although often stripped of all religious and ascetic trimmings. Such practices were often associated with a broad, inclusive and liberal spirituality. At the same time, on the opposite side of the spectrum, Hinduism was increasingly politicized.

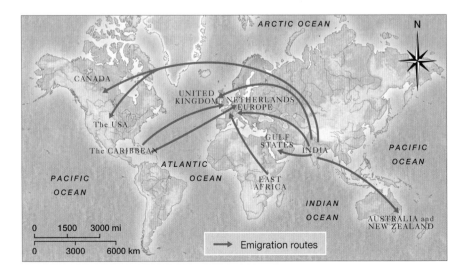

Above Hare Krishna devotees chant and dance in Boston in 1969, when Hindu thought was popular among the youth counter-culture.

INDIAN POLITICS

India's first Prime Minister, Jawaharlal Nehru, was succeeded in 1964 by Lal Bahadur Shastri, and two years later by Nehru's daughter, Indira Gandhi. In 1984, during her second term of office, Sikhs lobbied for their own state in the Punjab and militants entrenched themselves within their most holy site, the Golden Temple in Amritsar. Government troops stormed the complex, killing many Sikhs and outraging their community. Shortly afterward, Gandhi was assassinated by Sikh members of her personal bodyguard. Bloody retaliation further strained the previously cordial relationship between Sikhs and Hindus. Tensions also continued between Hindus and Muslims – and, in 1992, Hindus demolished the Babri Mosque in Ayodhya, provocatively built over Rama's birthplace. In the south, especially Kerala, conflict has repeatedly erupted over attempts to convert Hindus to Christianity, and over counter-measures to bring converts back to the Hindu fold.

HINDU IDENTITY

For Hindus, global contact with other faiths and cultures raised fresh questions over their identity. The very notion of Hinduism as a single religion appears relatively recent. Hindu nationalists claim otherwise, advocating that Hinduism, as a unified and cohesive religion, has long been inseparable from India, her people and her governance. Whilst nationalism advertises India as a Hindu country, an alternative current of thought promotes the universality of Hinduism, transcending sectarian borders.

The Hindu community is faced with many trying questions. Are hierarchical worldviews relevant to life today? Are caste and varnashrama now outdated? Should Hindu women play identical roles to men? Can Hindus, in good conscience, embrace embryonic and genetic research? How do the Hindu ideals of chivalrous kingship relate to terrorism, contemporary warfare and democratic leadership?

For many Hindus, their beliefs and practices remain a source of personal inspiration. Hindu texts almost unanimously agree that without inner tranquillity, human society seldom finds peace, prosperity and fulfilment, despite social and scientific progress. In trying to adapt its ancient wisdom to a quickly changing world, Hinduism faces many hurdles, and yet remains a vibrant, evolving and enriching tradition. Its enduring values, based on service, sustainability and the spiritual equality of all beings, may positively contribute to the key issues and debates of the contemporary world.

Below Indian Prime Minister Indira Gandhi, just months before her assassination in 1984, which exacerbated discord between Sikhs and Hindus.

CHAPTER 2

HOLY TEXTS

Many people are familiar with the Hindu book called the Bhagavad-gita, which relates a battlefield dialogue between Lord Krishna and his friend, Prince Arjuna. All the teachings of Hinduism were originally disseminated orally, and only later written down. Some traditions maintain that oral recitation constitutes the only legitimate mode of transmission.

The original Hindu canon is therefore called Shruti, 'that which is heard'. It consists largely of the four Vedas and their philosophical sub-sections called the Upanishads. These core texts are supplemented by a second category, which make the core texts more accessible. This category is called Smriti, 'that which is remembered'. A third category of texts, called Tantra, has variously been assimilated into both sections of Vedic literature, though the status of some texts remains disputed.

Most texts were originally taught in Sanskrit, and some draw primarily from ancient Tamil literature. For practical purposes today, the Bhagavad-gita is most important for understanding Hinduism's main philosophical concepts. As with most Vedic texts, it has been translated into hundreds of vernacular languages and usually includes a distinctive commentary by the author.

Opposite Hindu teachings are traditionally transmitted orally. In this Mughal miniature, Shukadeva narrates the Bhagavat Purana to King Parikshit and a group of sadhus.

Above A priest reads holy texts in Mathura, an ancient city of learning in the north Indian state of Uttar Pradesh.

PHILOSOPHY AND THEOLOGY

FOR REGULATING PRACTICE RATHER THAN BELIEF, HINDUISM IS CALLED 'A WAY OF LIFE'. DESPITE THIS, IT RIGOROUSLY ENGAGES WITH THEORY THROUGH MANY BRANCHES OF PHILOSOPHY AND THEOLOGY.

Hinduism has little experience of the schism between faith and reason that has typified Western intellectual history. Its religious life has tended toward reflection, and its philosophy toward practical application, especially the pursuit of liberation. Leaders rarely exhort followers to declare allegiance to a particular faith or creed. Indeed, Hindu texts define religion distinctively, as a process of knowledge. They explore moral issues largely in terms of 'knowledge versus ignorance', indicating a particular slant on the causes of good and evil. Above superficial belief, or even a sound intellectual understanding, Hinduism stresses the importance of direct experience, through self- and God-realization.

Many Hindus call their tradition 'Sanatana Dharma', the eternal order. The truths regarding the universal law were divinely revealed to ancient sages and for many aeons were transmitted orally. They were first written down much later, apparently around the start of the Kali-yuga, when human memory began to deteriorate. A sage called Vyasa (Badarayana) is generally accredited with writing many core texts, such as the Upanishads, Vedanta Sutras and the Mahabharata. Such books are presented today with extensive commentaries to help the reader grasp their real meaning.

As Hinduism developed, it did not reject its parent traditions, but modified and assimilated them into newer schools of thought. For example, the ancient Vedic notion of sacrifice, and the later philosophies of Sankhya and Yoga, have all been assimilated into the more recent school of Vedanta. Even the more exclusive lineages do not entirely reject 'other doctrines', but claim

Below A scene from the Mahabharata, with text written in Sanskrit. Story, rather than abstract philosophy, has helped transmit much popular Hinduism.

Above A brass murti of the great theologian called Ramanuja.

they demonstrate inferior understanding or are suitable for less spiritually mature practitioners.

THE SIX DARSHANAS

Despite a relatively inclusive approach, Hinduism has rejected doctrines that fail to acknowledge its scriptural authority. These include Jainism, Buddhism and the hedonistic philosophy of Charvaka. They are called 'nastika', differentiating them from the orthodox, 'astika' schools. However, 'Veda' literally means 'knowledge'. This generic meaning justifies the acceptance and assimilation of

HIGH AND LOW TRADITIONS

Textual scholarship is largely the preserve of the 'high', brahmin-led traditions. Much popular, village Hinduism engages little with philosophy, but is transmitted largely through custom and ritual.

There is a similar disparity between Hindu ideals and reality. Abortion is formally disapproved of but widely practised. The ideal of spiritual equality is advertised, but discredited by caste practice. However, these dichotomies do not imply that popular Hinduism is simply a degenerate form of the higher textual traditions; degeneracy may occur at any level, as illustrated by those brahmins who have taught and exploited a rigid caste-consciousness.

There has long been significant interplay between popular Hinduism and its high, Sanskrit-based traditions. Minor gods and goddesses are often elevated by reinforcing links to major deities. Villagers and everyday, working Hindus have, in some places, long been conversant with Hindu texts. Although Hinduism is 'a way of life', the impact of its philosophy and theology is pervasive.

one deals with theory and the other with the attendant practice and methodology. In this way, Sankhya forms the doctrinal basis for the discipline of Yoga; the atomic theory called Vaisheshika is grasped through Nyaya, logical debate; and Vedanta is the philosophy paired with the practice of ritual sacrifice. In reality though, the last pair have often locked horns, arguing for the supremacy of their respective practices and philosophies.

The precise age of the Six Darshanas is uncertain, though they date back at least to the Gupta period (240–550CE). Some groups consider them to be sequential, often with Vedanta as the culmination,

Above Students at a brahmin school, near Madurai in Tamil Nadu. The brahmin varna (class) was responsible for scriptural study and religious scholarship.

either chronologically or in terms of theological status. This is suggested by the fact that Vedanta means 'the end of the Vedas' or, less literally, 'the crown of knowledge'. Certainly, Vedanta today represents the more scholarly strands of Hinduism, and forms the doctrinal basis for most contemporary traditions.

Below Tree shrine dedicated to Kali in Andhra Pradesh, southern India. Much village practice shows little concern for Hindu scholarship.

auxiliary texts, such as the Tantras, if they support the Vedic conclusions. Hinduism recognizes that no one tradition, including its own, has a monopoly on spiritual truth.

There are six main astika systems, called Darshanas ('ways of seeing'). Although they are distinctive 'schools of thought', they are also complementary, representing different perspectives on identical truths. The various groups and sub-groups within Hinduism usually subscribe to one or more of the Six Darshanas. They are grouped as three pairs, or 'sisters'. Within each pair,

VAISHESHIKA AND NYAYA

HINDUISM'S RATIONAL APPROACH TO FAITH IS EXEMPLIFIED BY NYAYA
– THE DISCIPLINE OF LOGICAL DEBATE. ITS 'SISTER' DARSHANA,
VAISHESHIKA, RESEMBLES ONE SCHOOL OF GREEK PHILOSOPHY.

Vaisheshika falls within the broad philosophy called 'atomism' and was founded around 600BCE by a sage called Kanada. Legend states that he subsisted by collecting particles of grain (kana) scattered by the harvest, and earned the name Kana-bhuk, 'atom-eater'. He compiled the treatise called Vaisheshika Sutra, on which several commentaries were later written. Around the 11th century, Vaisheshika was closely associated with its 'sister school', Nyaya or 'the school of logic', but by the 15th century their combined influence had waned. In modern Hinduism, Nyaya forms the epistemological basis for rationale and

*Below Hindu scholars consulting texts.
Although Hinduism values logic and
human rationale, it also endorses
scriptural authority.*

philosophical thinking. Vaisheshika is relatively obscure, though modern Vedanta has adopted elements, such as its system for dividing and measuring time based on the movement of atomic particles.

VAISHESHIKA PHILOSOPHY

Similar to the Greeks, Kanada describes the elements, their characteristics and their interrelations. He classified all perceivable objects into six categories, to which a seventh category was later added. He propounded that all physical objects are reducible to a finite number of atoms and also postulated the existence of molecules. However, his philosophy is not a type of materialism, for he infers the existence of the eternal *atman*. To do this, however, he propounds a purely philosophical approach, accepting as

*Above An 18th-century bust of the
Greek philosopher Democritus, who
taught a form of atomism.*

valid only two sources of evidence, namely pratyaksha and anumana (empiricism and rationalism).

Despite a philosophical approach, Kanada endorses dharma as a means toward liberation, and prescribes traditional practices such as fasting, celibacy, and service to the guru. He further teaches that since all material objects are constructed from atoms, they are products, with the minute atoms themselves as causes. By introducing the principle of 'adrishta', a further, unknown and invisible cause, he opened the door for theistic doctrines, which proposed God as the remote and single cause of everything; he who orchestrates the innumerable atoms.

NYAYA

The school of logic known as Nyaya traces its origins to the disputations of Vedic scholars who cultivated debate as a sophisticated art, using the Upanishad as texts and developing notions of logical proof. The school of logic was more formally established by Akshapada Gautama. Born in the Himalayas around the

4th century BCE and systematized logic through books called the Nyaya Sutra. Thereafter, the school of Nyaya defined logic as a spiritual discipline aimed at apprehending truth and undermining the dishonest arguments that ensnare the soul.

The Navya-Nyaya (New School of Logic) developed from the 12th century and specialized in epistemology. As with Vaisheshika, it too accepted the need for sensory knowledge and inference, but added two further sources of evidence, namely *upamana* (analogy) and *shabda* ('sound' or scriptural testimony). Nyaya has also developed a sophisticated syllogism with five stages, rather like the three proposed by Aristotle. Distinctively, Nyaya texts philosophically argue for the existence of Ishvara (God), and many popular theistic schools still use its rationale arguments. Of the six Hindu systems, Nyaya enjoys the greatest respect from Western philosophers.

A FAMOUS DEBATE

One famous debate involved a young boy destined to become the great scholar called Yamunacharya. The contest took place between Yamuna and the king's proud chief advisor, Kolahala. The king and

queen were present and the queen favoured the young boy. The king confidently promised his wife that should Yamuna win, the boy would receive half the kingdom.

Yamuna put forward three statements and challenged his opponent to disprove them. He declared, 'First, your mother is not a barren woman: second, the king is supremely righteous: third, the queen is a model of chastity and faithfulness. Refute these if you can!'

Seeing the invitation to deny his own existence and to insult the king and queen, Kolahala squirmed in embarrassment and was stunned into silence. Visibly ruffled, he could only insist, as was formally required, that the boy refute his own propositions.

Yamuna calmly responded. 'The Manu Smriti states that one son is no son at all. You have no siblings and, therefore, in the eyes of scripture, your mother was barren.

Left Vaisheshika philosophy considers the atomic particle the absolute, indivisible truth.

Above Thousands of years ago, Sage Shukadeva instructed King Parikshit and a gathering of holy men. Discussion and debate are valued even outside the specific school of Nyaya (logic).

With regard for my second statement, the king accepts one sixth of his citizen's karma. In this materialistic age of Kali, people are more inclined to sin than piety. So the king, despite his own flawless character, is bearing a heavy burden of unrighteousness. As for the queen's chastity, holy texts applaud the monarch as the embodiment of all the demigods. Since the queen is also married to Indra, Agni, and Surya, how can she be called chaste?

As the court erupted in applause, Kolahala hung his head in shame. Yamuna won half the kingdom, but later renounced it for spiritual life, becoming the grand-guru of the famous theologian Ramanuja. The story teaches how logical thought is enhanced by humility and by knowledge derived from scriptural sources.

SANKHYA AND YOGA

THE OLDEST OF THE SIX DARSHANAS, SANKHYA, IS THE PHILOSOPHICAL FRAMEWORK UNDERPINNING THE PRACTICE OF YOGA, WHICH IS ESPECIALLY POPULAR AMONG THE ASCETIC, SHRAMANA TRADITIONS.

Sankhya is attributed to the sage Kapila who lived around 700BCE. Some scholars claim that there were two Kapilas, teaching theistic and non-theistic versions of the same doctrine. Sankhya is a system of metaphysics based upon a subtle and sophisticated analysis of causation. To modern Hindu thought, Sankhya contributes the notion of individual agency, by which the soul creates its unique destiny by generating successive material bodies. By reversing this process, by sequentially peeling away layers of material coverings, the practice of Yoga aims to reveal the real, eternal self.

SANKHYA

The term Sankhya means 'number' or 'to count', and refers to a philosophical system of analysing matter. It aims to overcome suffering through discernment, thus releasing the soul, called the enjoyer (purusha), from its entanglement in matter (praktiti). It is highly dualistic,

based on apprehending the difference between spirit (Brahman) and matter (prakriti).

Sankhya was originally non-theistic, classifying 24 material 'truths' or elements. The soul became the 25th element. Theistic schools later added a 26th element called the parama-purusha, the 'supreme-enjoyer' (God). The later Tantric notion of Shiva-Shakti is similar to the purusha-prakriti model. Shiva is the male, the energetic, and Shakti the complementary female energy. The Vedanta schools, through texts such as the Bhagavad-gita, also assimilated many of the terms and concepts of Sankhya. A particularly important contribution is the idea of three gunas, the material qualities that permeate and regulate matter.

Significantly, Sakhya's framework applies to both the structure of the universe and the psycho-physical form of the living being. For both cosmos and creature, creation begins with the subtle and proceeds to the gross. This reveals the agency

Above A sadhu (Indian holy man) performing hatha-yoga outdoors in India. Sadhus followsa strict, regulated lifestyle, free of sensual distraction.

that spirit exhibits over matter. For the soul (atman), the first causal layer is false ego – 'identification with matter' – followed by intelligence, and thereafter mind. Mind generates ether, the first and finest of the five gross elements. The other four elements are generated in turn, culminating in earth. Each of the five gross elements has a corresponding perceptive sense and a sense-object; additionally, there are five 'working senses' or instruments of action.

Below A woman sits in a meditative pose at a yoga school in the USA, where the practice is adopted mainly for health and relaxation.

THE EIGHT STEPS OF YOGA

Astanga-yoga means the yoga of eight 'limbs' or steps, which are progressive and culminate in samadhi ('fixed-mind'), the final stage of yoga when the mind is focused on one point:

Yama – restraints and prohibitions
Niyama – positive observances
Asana – physical postures
Pranayama – regulation of breath
Pratyahara – sensory withdrawal
Dharana – concentration
Dhyana – meditation
Samadhi – complete absorption

Above Sage Kapila instructing his mother in Sankhya philosophy, which underpins traditional yoga practice.

THE 24 ELEMENTS OF SANKHYA PHILOSOPHY

1 Pradhana — The Pradhana is the unmanifest three gunas (goodness, passion and ignorance).

Three Subtle Elements — The three subtle elements constitute the subtle (astral) body, and the five gross elements
2 False-ego — constitute the outward body. They are listed here in order from subtle to gross. The living
3 Intelligence — being has five knowledge-acquiring senses and five working senses, each of which
4 Mind — corresponds to one of the five elements and the corresponding sense-objects.

Five Gross Elements	Five Sense Objects	Five Perceptive Senses	Five Working Senses
5 Ether	10 Sound	15 Ear	20 Voice
6 Air	11 Touch	16 Skin	21 Legs
7 Fire	12 Sight	17 Eye	22 Arms
8 Water	13 Taste	18. Tongue	23 Reproductive organs
9 Earth	14 Smell	19 Nose	24 Evacuating organs

ASTANGA-YOGA

Yoga, the discipline of meditation, is intimately linked to Sankhya. It is also termed 'raja-yoga', indicating its perceived pre-eminence as 'the king of yogas', or 'Patanjali-yoga', after its founder. Sage Patanjali is considered an incarnation of Shesha, Vishnu's celestial serpent, and probably lived around the 2nd century BCE. His texts, the Patanjali Sutras, consist of 194 aphorisms divided into four padas (sections): samadhi (trance), sadhana (practice), vibhuti (mystic powers) and kaivalya (oneness), the ultimate aim.

The process itself is divided into eight limbs or 'angas'. Although popular hatha-yoga is related to astanga-yoga, the exercises in Patanjali's system are designed not for physical health, but to facilitate meditation and self-realization. Hatha-yoga enables the yogi to sit comfortably, without strain or slumber, and to exercise control over the breath. Patanjali warns the yogi not to be allured by the eight mystic siddhis (perfections), such as the ability to become 'smaller than the smallest' or to materialize objects from distant places. Rather, the yogi

should remain fixed on the goal of directly discerning the eternal self, consistent with Sankhya philosophy.

Additionally, the yogi should purge himself of base qualities, such as lust, greed and anger, and develop complete mastery over mind and senses. Patanjali also recommends scriptural study and surrender to the Lord, which bestow peace,

illumination and samadhi. *Kaivalya* refers to the realization that one is not the body but the soul within. It is achieved when the yogi is fixed in meditation on God within and no longer influenced by the prompting of the three gunas (material qualities). Many principles of Yoga and Sankhya have been integrated into popular theistic and devotional Hinduism.

Right Women practising yoga in the ruins of Bhangarh, a city built by the Jaipur royal family in the 1500s.

MIMAMSA AND VEDANTA

THESE SISTER SCHOOLS ARE ALSO CALLED PURVA MIMAMSA (EARLY INQUIRY) AND UTTARA MIMAMSA (LATER INQUIRY). VEDANTA REPRESENTS MUCH CONTEMPORARY HINDU THOUGHT.

Above Mimamsa stresses adherence to duty (dharma) and the brahmin-led performance of ritual, especially the fire sacrifice, conducted here in Oxford, UK.

Mimamsa and Vedanta correspond to two main classifications within the Vedas, namely the karma-kanda (action section) and the jnana-kanda (knowledge section). They deal respectively with ritual and philosophy, and the corresponding concepts of dharma (duty) and Brahman (the absolute reality). Purva Mimamsa is largely associated with the early Vedic period and the brahmin-led, householder and sacrificial traditions intent on worldly and celestial enjoyment. Vedanta developed later, both as a complementary school and a counter-movement, stressing puja (worship), mysticism and liberation though renunciation. Vedanta had a pervasive influence on the intellectual and religious life of India, and remains the most prestigious school.

Below A boy studies the Upanishads, the section of the Vedas teaching Vedanta philosophy.

MIMAMSA

'Investigation' or Mimamsa is the earliest of the six darshanas, providing the ideas behind Vedic sacrifice and the first rules for textual interpretation. The inaugural text, the Mimamsa-sutra, is attributed to Rishi Jaimini, who lived around the 4th century BCE as the disciple of Vyasa, author of the Mahabharata. Jaimini's inaugural teachings were developed by a long line of commentators; first, Sabara (*c.*150CE), and then, around the 8th century, Kumarila Bhatta and Prabhakara Mishra. From 400 until 900CE, the school dominated Hindu thought.

Mimamsa explored the interpretation and explanation of scripture, it also fostered the study of philology, the philosophy of language. It also spawned theories of 'sacred sound', first consolidated by Bhartrihari, the 7th-century Sanskrit grammarian. Mimamsa is largely atheistic, or at least agnostic. It demanded diligent, almost mechanistic practice and the perfect intonation of mantras (incantations), with little emphasis on the underlying mood or attitude. To achieve happiness, it advocated the unfailing success of properly executed dharma (duty), rather than divine intervention by an independent, benevolent God.

From the turn of the first millennium, scholars such as Bopadeva developed theistic stands of Mimamsa, but the darshana was gradually eclipsed by the burgeoning school of Vedanta. Today two traditions survive; the Bhattas and the Prabhakaras, following Kumarila Bhatta and Prabhakara Mishra respectively. Much modern Hinduism has retained Mimamsa prayers, and rituals like the fire sacrifice, usually assimilating them within a theistic, Vedantic framework.

VEDANTA

The later Mimamsa school is usually called Vedanta, meaning either 'the end of knowledge', referring to its later development, or 'the crown of knowledge', indicating its perceived superiority. It expounds upon the Vedic notion of Brahman (the absolute) and derives philosophical impetus from the Upanishads and Vedanta Sutras. Vedanta philosophy is accredited to the sage and author Vyasa who traditionally goes back

to the Mahabharata era. Vedanta came to the fore with Shankara (780–812CE), who revitalized interest in the Vedas and hastened the decline of Buddhism within southern Asia. For Shankara, spiritual liberation was achieved not by ritual action but by knowledge.

Vedantic schools revere scripture, or 'shabda', as the most authentic form of evidence (pramana). Sensory perception (pratyaksha) and logical inference (anumana) are also accepted but, being fallible, are accountable to scriptural standards. While recognizing limitations to the mind and senses, Vedanta asserts the eternal self's capacity, once enlightened, to perceive spirit. By controlling and purifying the mind and senses, the boundaries of perception can be extended to embrace the spiritual.

To be accepted as a genuine Vedantic school, a lineage must present commentaries on three scriptures: the Upanishads, the Vedanta Sutras and the Bhagavadgita, collectively called the 'prasthana trayi'. Some books list ten authentic

Below Vivekananda sitting in meditation. He pursued the advaita school of Vedanta, teaching about an impersonal Supreme.

Above Some schools of Vedanta favour a personal God. Madhva (1197–1276) taught a dualistic philosophy and the worship of Krishna, who is shown here.

schools of Vedanta. After Shankara's 'monism', most important were the theologies of Ramanuja ('qualified monism') and Madhva ('pure dualism'). Ramanuja (1017–1137) qualified Shankara's monism, holding that salvation is attained neither though ritual nor knowledge, but devotion (bhakti) to a personal God. More firmly than Ramanuja before him, Madhva (1197–1276) contested Shakara's monism by asserting rigid and permanent distinctions between the self, God and matter.

MODERN VEDANTA

Well into the 20th century, many commentators saw Shankara's monistic doctrine as the epitome of Indian intellectual achievement. They thought Advaita synonymous with Vedanta. Recent awareness of devotional scholarship has promoted interest in alternative, theistic perspectives and recognition of those branches of Vedanta advocating a personal Supreme. Many of the large global movements, such as ISKCON (the Hare Krishna Movement), the Swaminarayana lineages and the Ramakrishna Mission draw from Vedanta philosophy.

Vedanta is most favoured by two communities: Vaishnavism and Shankara's Advaita branch of the Smarta tradition. Amongs Shaivas, Vedanta is less central, though still intimately linked to the Shaiva Siddhanta traditions through a theologian called Shrikantha. For Shaktas, Vedanta is even less relevant, although Vivekananda attempted to establish links through his 'neo-Vedanta' adaptation of Shankara's Advaita. However, some forms of Advaita, such as Kashmiri Shaivism, are not forms of Vedanta but derive from Tantric texts. Even so, Vedanta dominates modern Hindu thought, and it has absorbed many ideas from the other Darshanas.

THE MAIN SACRED TEXTS

FOR MANY HINDUS, THE CORE OF THEIR TRADITION IS LOCATED WITHIN SPECIFIC HOLY TEXTS, THE VEDAS AND THEIR SUPPLEMENTS. DISTINCTIVE TO HINDUISM IS THE VAST NUMBER OF TEXTS.

The concept of Hinduism as a single monolithic religion is recent, dating back only to the 19th century. Hence, any definition of Hinduism remains somewhat arbitrary and provisional. Some followers prefer the alternative name, 'Vaidika Dharma', referring to those who follow the teachings outlined in the Vedas. These sacred books are certainly pivotal, and along with their corollary texts are collectively called 'the Vedic literature'.

SHRUTI AND SMRITI

The Vedic literature is divided into two main parts, called the Shruti ('that which has been heard') and the Smriti ('that which has been remembered'). Shruti, comprised of the four Vedas, connotes revealed, infallible and eternal truth. On the other hand, Smriti is supplementary, changes over time, and is authorized for conforming to the bedrock of truth found in Shruti. There are different opinions about the relative importance of each. Some Hindus stress the canonical importance of Shruti, whereas others consider Smriti equally important for making abstract truths more accessible.

The word Veda literally means 'knowledge'. The connotation of universal Truth, in contrast to exclusive belief, implies that any teaching consistent with the Veda may be accepted as 'Veda', legitimate knowledge. Hence, numerous writings have been assimilated into the Smriti, including vernacular works whose prominence is limited to a specific tradition or geographical region. A third block of literature,

Above The Shruti and Smriti were first transmitted orally and later also in writing, mainly in the Devanagari characters of Sanskrit, as in this late 19th-century scroll.

called Tantra, has its original source beyond Shruti and Smriti, but is accepted for its broad resonance with Vedic conclusions. Although many Tantras (also called Agamas) have been widely incorporated into the Vedic canon, the status and legitimacy of some remain contested.

DIVISIONS OF CONTENT

The content of texts, specifically the Shruti, is divided into two main divisions, namely karma-kanda, dealing with world-affirming ritual, and jnana-kanda, philosophical texts aimed at knowledge through world abnegation. Some traditions add a third category called upasana-kanda, denoting the worship section and, for some, a view that the world should be neither wholeheartedly embraced nor rigidly renounced.

Left Late 20th-century French version of the Bhagavat Purana, part of the Smriti, venerated on a shrine at a Belgian theological college.

Above Texts are used for personal study. Here an Indian man inspects a volume at a temple bookshop.

The three sections correlate to the paths of karma (action), jnana (knowledge) and bhakti (devotion). Metaphorically, in relation to the human form, karma-kanda represents the limbs, jnana-kanda the head and upasana-kanda the heart. Philosophical debates most often revolve around the precise relationship between head and heart, and the relative roles of knowledge and devotion.

LANGUAGE

Early texts were written in classical Sanskrit, which translates as 'the most refined language'. The script itself is termed 'devanagari', signifying an exalted language spoken in 'the cities of the gods'. Sanskrit has often been the preserve of the learned, brahminical class, and ordinary folk spoke a variety of Prakrits, or 'natural languages', featuring Sanskrit roots but a simplified grammar. The non-Vedic, non-orthodox movements, such as Jainism and Buddhism, adopted Prakrits as their own sacred languages.

In parts of South India, Tamil has achieved a similar status to Sanskrit as a sacred language. Some lineages, particularly the Shri Vaishnavas, have amalgamated both linguistic traditions. Many subsidiary texts, particularly those by medieval bhakti writers, were written in local vernaculars, such as Avanti, Gujarati, Bengali, Telegu and Kannada. They are still used today. Many texts have been translated into non-Indian tongues, and there are continuing debates over how important a primary language is to the authentic transmission of Hindu teachings.

HOW TEXTS ARE USED

Ancient texts were transmitted orally and later written on leaves, such as palm. Today, printed and bound books are sturdier but still treated with great respect. They are never placed directly on the floor or touched with the feet or grubby hands, and may be wrapped in silk. Prayers are often recited before their use in public recitation, scholarly study and religious discourse (pravachana). They may be consulted on matters of spiritual and secular law. Today, the philosophically abstruse Vedas are studied mainly by scholars, whereas the Smriti texts are more widely used.

Below Scriptural verses identify a theme for religious lectures, as delivered by this sadhu at the BAPS Swaminarayana Temple in Neasden, London.

MAIN SHRUTI TEXTS	MAIN SMRITI TEXTS
The Four Vedas: 1 Rig Veda 2 Yajur Veda 3 Sama Vada 4 Atharva Veda	**The Vedanta Sutra** (codes of philosophy, the essence of Hindu theology) **The Two Epics** (or Itihasas, 'histories') (a) the Ramayana ('the journey of Rama', the shorter of the two epics) (b) the Mahabharata ('the history of Greater India', the longest known poem)
The 108 Upanishads (philosophical texts)	**The Bhagavad-gita** (philosophical part of the Mahabharata)
	The Puranas (literally 'very old', story and 'myth')
The Six Vedangas (skills to study/apply the Vedas)	**The Dharma Shastra** (law books and moral codes)

THE VEDAS AND UPANISHADS

THE FOUR VEDAS ARE PERHAPS THE OLDEST HINDU TEXTS. THE UPANISHADS ARE KEY SECTIONS DEALING WITH VEDANTA PHILOSOPHY BASED ON THE CORE NOTION OF AN ABSOLUTE REALITY.

The Vedas were compiled over an extended period beginning about 2,500 years ago, though the tradition often considers them older. Pinning down dates is problematic, for two main reasons.

First, the teachings were originally conveyed orally and only later written and re-written over extended periods, and by several authors. Second, there are different opinions, especially between Western academics and Hindus themselves. Adherents propound earlier dates and some teach that the Shruti should be heard only and never transmitted in written form. Tradition suggests that there was originally one Vedic lore, subse-

Above In front of his small shrine, a priest reads a modern translation of the four Vedas.

quently divided into the four Vedas. Western scholars consider the Rig Veda the oldest.

THE FOUR VEDAS

The Rig Veda is certainly the most important of the Vedas. Divided into ten books, or '*mandalas*', it includes 1,028 hymns in praise of 'the Vedic' deities such as Indra, Agni, Rudra, Vishnu, and Varuna. It contains two central Hindu prayers: the famous Gayatri mantra, chanted thrice daily by brahmins, and the Purusha Shukta, narrating the story of creation from the purusha, the 'cosmic man' later associated with Vishnu.

The Yajur Veda is a handbook for priests in their performance of yajnas (sacrifices) and has two parts: the earlier 'black' section and the later 'white' section. The Sama Veda consists of chants and melodies for use during *yajna*. Unlike the former three Vedas, the Atharva Veda deals little with sacrifice, but contains hymns and incantations for protection from evil, achievement of life's various aims, and performance of rites of passage.

FOUR SECTIONS

Within each of the four books there are four types of composition. Some claim that only the first represents the 'true Vedas'. The first two divisions comprise the karma-kanda (ritual section) and relate to the performance of the sacrifices at the heart of the Mimamsa school. The second pair correspond to the jnana-kanda (the knowledge section), expounding the philosophy dear to the Vedanta schools. Some writers have suggested that the four sections, moving progressively toward detachment, correspond to the four ashramas, namely student life, household life, retirement and renunciation of the world.

UPANISHADS

The word Upanishad, 'sitting near', alludes to ancient tutorials in which students humbly sat at the guru's feet.

Below The Jagadambi Temple at Khadjuraho, built on architectural principles outlined in the Upavedas, specifically the Shilpa-veda.

Often considered the start of direct spiritual instruction, the Upanishads outline core teachings about the atman, reincarnation, karma and liberation. The traditional number is 108, though there are far more, including many of recent origin. However, 13 are considered principal. Of particular importance is the Svetashvatara Upanishad,

Below A painting used for the cover of a popular version of one of the main Upanishads, the Shri Ishopanishad, which alludes to a personal Supreme.

which, for Shaiva traditions, has attained a canonical status similar to the Bhagavad-gita. Although the Gita is technically part of the Smriti, for its eminence as a philosophical text it has been alternatively named the Gitopanishad.

VEDANTA SUTRAS
The word sutra literally means 'thread', referring to a code or aphorism that can be unwound indefinitely to reveal layer upon layer of truth. Using such codes, many voluminous texts on diverse topics were condensed into smaller books, also called sutras. They include the Dharma Sutras, summarizing religious and secular law, the Shrauta Sutras dealing with public sacrifice, and the Grihya Sutras, providing a summary of domestic rites. Most important, though, are the philosophical 'Vedanta Sutras'.

Sage Vyasa wrote the Vedanta Sutras, or the Brahma Sutras, to systematize the diverse teachings strewn throughout the Upanishads. Unlike the Upanishads, they belong to the Smriti. However, within Vedanta, they are attributed to a unique, third section called Nyaya (logic), thus creating the prashthan trayi (three canonical texts). The Upanishads are Shruti, the Bhagavad-gita is Smriti, and the

Above Students at a Gujarat school listen to their guru, Rameshbai Oza, who sits on the traditional and honorific raised seat. Upanishad literally means 'sitting near'.

Brahma Sutras are Nyaya. Various scholars wrote lengthy commentaries on these three to establish the different schools of Vedanta. However, because people are less philosophically adept in the modern age, the Upanishads and Vedanta Sutra are often inaccessible without the guidance of the Smriti literature, which includes history, story and myth, and moral guidelines.

SOUTH INDIAN LITERARY TRADITIONS

IN INDIA, THE NORTHERN AND SOUTHERN CULTURES AND TRADITIONS ARE SOMEWHAT DIFFERENT. SOUTH INDIANS ARE CALLED DRAVIDIANS, DIFFERENTIATING THEM FROM THE NORTHERN ARYANS.

Southern India has been less prone to invasion, occupation and assimilation of foreign influence. Differences with the north extend to linguistic, textual and scholarly heritages. As Sanskrit is widely considered a sacred language, Tamil has acquired a similar status in the south. Tamil texts can wield authority equal to the Vedas. Other southern languages, widely used for translating standard texts, have been less influential.

THE SANGAM LITERATURE

Tamil literature goes back to the remote past and three ancient assemblies (Sangams) of poets and scholars. Legend suggests that the earliest conventions were attended by deities such as Shiva and Murugan, and were based at Madurai or, according

Below Women carry water from the Tungabhadra River, Hampi. South Indian literature drew rich, sensual metaphor from the lush southern landscape.

to some accounts, a fabled continent later swallowed by the sea. The earliest surviving Sangam literature dates from between 300BCE and 200CE. Its themes are largely secular and world-affirming, comparing the various human emotions to lush forest, towering mountains and other features of the luxuriant South Indian landscape.

DEVOTIONAL TEXTS

The rich aesthetic themes continued in the copious outpourings of the Alvars and Nayanmars, the devotional poets of the first millennium CE. The Nayanmar hymns dedicated to Shiva comprise a 12-book anthology called the Thirumurai. It includes a treatise on yoga by Rishi Thirumular. The hymns of the first seven books, collectively called the Thevaram, were set to music and remain part of contemporary temple liturgy. Legend holds that the abandoned Thirumurai texts were discovered by

Above The giant statue of Saint Valluvar. His three raised fingers symbolize the key texts he wrote.

the Chola king, Rajaraja the First (r. 985–1014CE) and subsequently classified by a scholar named Nampi.

A further core text is the Thirukural, three books written in couplets (kurals) by St Thiruvalluvar. The books correspond to the first three of the four aims of human life outlined in Sanskrit texts. The first book explores *aram*, similar to the Sanskrit 'dharma', meaning 'duty'; the second is on *porul* or in Sanskrit 'artha', meaning prosperity; and the third on *inbam*, in Sanskrit 'kama', indicating sensual pleasure. At the southern tip of India a 133-feet (40.5m) tall statue of Thiruvalluvar has been carved out of rock. His height symbolizes the 133 chapters in his text, and his three straight fingers denote the themes of aram, porul and inbam.

SYNTHESIZING TRADITIONS

Tradition credits Nathamuni with recovering the lost hymns of the Vaishnava saints, the 12 Alvars. Nathamuni arranged these songs in canonical form and revived the practice of reciting them before the temple deity. In South India, the 4,000 verses are called the Valayiram

Above Brahmin priests, largely responsible for scholarship, officiate at a wedding in Kanchipuram.

('Four Thousand') in Tamil and the Divya Prabhandham ('Divine Composition') in Sanskrit. They are considered equal to the Vedas, and hence called 'the Dravidian Veda' or 'the Tamil Veda'. In many temples, the chanting of the Divya Prabhandham forms a major part of the daily service and the Shri Vaishnava tradition continues the recitation of both Tamil and Sanskrit texts.

After the collapse of the northern Gupta dynasty around 400CE, Hinduism's greatest strides were made in South India, hastening the decline of Jainism and Buddhism. The great theologian Shankara, who was born around 780CE, started the first important lineage of Vedanta philosophy, preaching Advaita or 'non-dualism'. Ramanuja (1017–1137CE) modified Shankara's doctrine to propose that God is ultimately a person. Ramanuja's theology, infused with the sentiment of the Alvars, helped to fire the Vaishnava devotional traditions that engulfed India between 1200 and 1700CE. His theology may have significantly influenced southern Shaiva devotion, particularly the Shaiva Advaita school. Many of Hinduism's greatest theologians came from south India, contesting the ideas of Aryan, northern supremacy and of a rigid divide between the two cultures.

MEDIEVAL LITERATURE
Basavanna (1134–1196), born in what is now Karnataka state, rejected the brahmin hierarchy and started the first devotional movement, the Lingayats. During the same period, many 'sthala purana's (temple histories) were written, tracing the history of each religious building and its deity. There emerged several Tamil works in honour of specific deities, such as Murugan. However, not all texts honoured such deities. Kambhan wrote a Tamil version of the Ramayana, in which – some claim – he reverses the values, glorifying the Dravidian hero Ravana pitted against the evil, invading Aryans led by Rama.

HINDUISM IN SRI LANKA
The Ramayana contains perhaps the earliest reference to Sri Lanka, off the south-eastern corner of India. It recounts the invasion of Ravana's kingdom by Rama's army of monkeys, setting a precedent for a history punctuated by coups, conquests and ethnic tension. Today, a declining 15 per cent of the populace are Hindu, mainly following folk customs such as fire-walking, animal sacrifice and possession by local gods, with minimal reference to scholarly traditions. Worship of minor deities, such as Kannaki, is often based on ancient and unique Tamil epics. Upper-class Tamils largely adhere to the Shaiva Siddhanta lineage. Their temples observe rituals based on the Sanskritized Agama (Tantric) texts, along with the recitation of Tamil hymns by specialized singers called Oduvar, representing further synthesis of southern and Sanskritic traditions.

Below A figure on the tower of a temple in Colombo. In Sri Lanka, Hinduism is represented mainly by South Indian folk tradition and the scholarly Shaiva Siddhanta lineage.

THE RAMAYANA

'THE JOURNEY OF RAMA', OR THE RAMAYANA, IS A SANSKRIT EPIC OF 24,000 VERSES. IT IS THE EARLIER AND SHORTER OF THE TWO HINDU EPIC POEMS: THE OTHER IS THE MAHABHARATA.

The Ramayana was compiled by the poet-sage Valmiki, who may have lived around the 4th century BCE. Tradition dates him far earlier. Scholars believe that the Valmiki Ramayana received its present shape as late as the 2nd century CE, though it contains much older material.

The text survives in many partial and complete manuscripts, the oldest dating from the 11th century CE. Though academics consider the Ramayana a mythical account, many Hindus consider Rama an historical figure, and date him back to the silver age, the Treta-yuga.

Above A modern painting of Rama, Sita and Lakshmana after Rama's banishment to the Dandakaranya forest.

SUMMARY OF THE STORY
Prince Rama was the eldest of four sons begotten by Dasharatha, King of Koshala. Just prior to Dasharatha's retirement and Rama's coronation, the prince was unfairly banished to the forest. His wife Sita and brother Lakshmana joined him. Despite the hardships, Rama relished forest life, for it allowed him to keep company with the saints and sages living there.

However, Ravana, king of the race of Rakshasas (man-eaters), heard of Sita's exquisite beauty and resolved to kidnap her. He conspired with the magician Maricha, who adopted the form of a delicate deer. As planned, it captivated Sita's mind and Rama set out to catch the playful yet elusive creature. Maricha also lured away Lakshmana. Ravana seized the unprotected Sita. Whisking her off on his aerial chariot to his capital, Lanka, he held her captive in his famed Ashoka garden.

Finding Sita gone, Rama was grief-stricken. Pacified by Lakshmana, he resolved to rescue his wife. Journeying south with determination,

Left This carving in a Balinese temple depicts how Maricha took the form of a deer to lure Rama away from Sita.

Above A modern rendition of the triumphant return to Ayodhya of Rama and Sita after their army defeated Ravana.

the brothers allied themselves with Sugriva, king of a race of monkey-like people. Sugriva's general, Hanuman, eventually found Sita on the isle of Lanka, but was detected by Ravana's son, Indrajit, and rewarded with a lighted tail. Hanuman escaped and, waving his famous tail, burned down most of the splendid city before bounding back to the Indian mainland.

Hearing of Sita's whereabouts, Rama ordered his army to toss giant boulders into the sea. Miraculously they floated, and the monkey warriors constructed a pontoon bridge extending to Lanka. The two armies clashed outside the city. Rama's troops gained the upper hand, and eventually Rama killed Ravana. Reunited, Rama and Sita returned to Ayodhya, where they reigned happily for many years.

However, due to a malicious rumour, Rama banished Sita to the ashrama of sage Valmiki, where she bore twin sons, Lava and Kusha. Years later, Sita and her two teenage princes briefly met Rama, though

Right A performance of the Ramayana in Java, Indonesia, where the story remains extremely popular.

the couple never reunited. In separation from Rama, Sita ended her life by entering the earth and, when Rama also departed, their two sons inherited the kingdom.

MEANING OF THE STORY

The story is interpreted from different perspectives. In the worldly sense, it describes Indian society at the time and the Hindu ideal of chivalrous kingship. It extols the virtues of worldly dharma (duty), of loyalty to family members, and of a powerful leadership that transcends personal ambition. It also shows the karmic consequences of lust and avarice, as embodied by Ravana. For some renouncer traditions, it illustrates the difficulties encountered when getting married.

On a higher lever, the story describes the eternal lila (spiritual pastimes) of the seventh avatara of Vishnu. Especially through the examples of Sita's chastity and Hanuman's service, it illustrates the virtues of devotion, surrender to God, and his saving grace. A much-quoted couplet, spoken by Rama, translates: 'If a person just once surrenders to me, sincerely saying, "My Lord, from this day I am yours", then from that point on I always give him protection. That is my vow.'

THE RAMAYANA IN ART

Over time, the message of the Valmiki Ramayana has been transmitted mainly through its vernacular versions, notably a Tamil version and the much-loved Hindi 'Ramcharitmanas' by Tulsidas. The Ramayana, with its elements of hero-worship, has been expressed and transmitted through such art forms as poetry, dance and drama; and, more recently, film and television. Its cultural transmission has allowed it to blend with other faith traditions. A Jain version exalts Rama not as an avatara of Vishnu but as a liberated soul.

The popularity of the Ramayana is most conspicuous in South-east Asia, with its numerous versions, such as the Thai 'Ramakien' and the Javanese 'Kakawin Ramayana', popularly performed through ballet. Scenes for the story also feature in bas-relief and sculpture, as in the Cambodian temple at Angkor Wat, or in Thailand, where huge statues of Sugriva and other characters decorate the courtyard of the royal palace. Ramayana sculptures also adorn the walls and balustrades of Buddhist temples, where some regard Rama as an avatara of the Buddha. Through its various artistic expressions, the story of Rama and Sita is also increasingly well-known to the Western world.

THE MAHABHARATA

THIS SECOND HINDU EPIC CONSISTS OF 100,000 COUPLETS, MAKING IT ONE OF THE LONGEST POEMS IN THE WORLD. MAHABHARATA MEANS 'THE HISTORY OF GREATER INDIA'.

According to tradition, the Mahabharata was originally narrated by sage Vyasa and written down by the elephant-headed Ganesha. Its composition may have undergone various stages. The intricate and multi-layered plot focuses on the political tensions between the five Pandavas and their 100 cousins, the Kauravas. Its climax is a detailed description of the fratricidal battle of Kurukshetra. Woven within the epic are many other historical tales, and several philosophical discourses, including the Bhagavad-gita. The text particularly explores the intricacies and ambiguities of dharma, especially for the priestly and warrior classes, and the decline in virtue that marked the end of an era.

SUMMARY OF THE STORY

Pandu was the second of three princes but ascended the throne due to the blindness of his elder brother, Dhritarashtra. Pandu died prematurely, leaving a wife and five young sons. His younger brother, Vidura,

Below Krishna supplies endless cloth to Draupadi as a Kaurava prince tries to disrobe her.

Above Arjuna successfully takes aim during the marriage contest, thus winning the hand of Princess Draupadi.

was the son of a maid-servant and disqualified from taking the throne. Subsequently, the court elders decided that Dhritarashtra should act as regent until rule rightfully passed to Pandu's sons, headed by Yudhisthira. However, as all the princes grew up, Dhritarashtra's 100 sons, headed by Duryodhana, were increasingly resentful that fate had deprived their family of the vast Indian empire.

They conspired to assassinate their cousins, the teenage Pandavas and their widowed mother, Kunti. However, the princes were warned, and escaped a burning wax palace via a pre-prepared tunnel. Now fully aware of their cousins' treachery, they chose to remain in the forest and to be considered dead. During this time, the third brother, Arjuna, won Draupadi as his bride during an archery contest. Due to a benediction from Lord Shiva, awarded in a previous life, Draupadi became the wife of all five brothers.

News eventually reached the blind Dhritarashtra that his nephews were still alive. Relieved of his guilt, and feeling repentant, he arranged to return half the kingdom to the Pandavas, though by far the worst

Above Troops prepare for the Battle of Kurukshetra, in a 12th-century bas-relief at the Cambodian Angkor Wat temple.

half. With the divine help of Krishna, the barren lands flourished and the kingdom became fabulously wealthy. Hearing news of Yudhisthira's fame, opulence and popularity, Duryodhana seethed with envy. He threatened and cajoled his blind and affectionate father to schedule a gambling match between the two groups of cousins.

Duryodhana devised that the dice be loaded. Yudhisthira lost everything, including his wife and brothers. At Duryodhana's behest, his brother Dussasana tried to disrobe Draupadi before the royal court, but Krishna protected her dignity by supplying an endless length of saree. None of the nobles intervened, and according to the law of karma, sowed the seeds of their inevitable destruction. There and then, the five brothers took terrible and irrevocable oaths to destroy the offenders. None the less, according to the terms of a gambling match, they were exiled to the forest for a further 13 years. As a condition, if they were

Right A scene from the 18-day battle. Krishna, impelled by affection for Arjuna, lifts a chariot wheel and almost breaks his vow to abstain from fighting.

discovered during the final and 13th year, they were to remain in exile for a further 12 years.

Thus the princes and their wife again entered the forest. After many adventures, they adopted disguises for the final year, marginally avoiding detection by the spies dispatched by their cousins. When they returned to reclaim their kingdom, the Kauravas bluntly refused. Duryodhana repeatedly thwarted Krishna's peace proposals, and so the two parties arrayed their troops on the plains of Kurukshetra. After 18 days of carnage, the Pandavas emerged victorious due to the presence and guidance of Lord Krishna.

Yudhisthira was crowned emperor, and his kingdom prospered for 36 years. With Lord Krishna's demise, the five Pandavas retired to the Himalayas, leaving Arjuna's grandson on the throne.

THE POPULARITY OF THE MAHABHARATA

The Mahabharata is a favourite subject of art and drama, and it is still tremendously popular in India and beyond, particularly in Indonesia. One specific version survives on the island of Java, and the relief work at the temple at Angkor Wat in Cambodia depicts many scenes from the story. One TV version, screened in the early 1990s, was so popular that it practically brought the whole of India to a halt. The story has also won the attention of Western directors such as Peter Brook, who staged a six-hour version in the 1980s. Tradition holds that the intrigue, romance and chivalry are especially meant to capture the attention of people in Kali-yuga, who prefer entertainment to philosophy. None the less, the message of the Mahabharata is ultimately spiritual, and at the heart of the epic is the Bhagavad-gita, narrated as the two armies stood poised for battle.

THE BHAGAVAD-GITA: SONG OF GOD

THE BEST-KNOWN HINDU SCRIPTURE WORLDWIDE, THE BHAGAVAD-GITA OR 'SONG OF GOD', PRESENTS A BROAD OUTLINE OF HINDU PHILOSOPHY, INCLUDING ALL THE MAIN CONCEPTS AND VALUES.

Above Hindus in Auckland, New Zealand, recite the Bhagavad-gita during the Gita Jayanti festival, which falls in December.

The Bhagavad-gita consists of 700 verses within 18 chapters. According to tradition, it was spoken around 3,000BCE, though scholars consider it more recent, dating its present form to *c.* 200CE. As part of the Mahabharata, it is technically a Smriti literature, but some have attempted to raise its status to Shruti by calling it the 'Gita-Upanishad'. There are now thousands of editions, translated into all major languages and usually published with extensive commentary illuminating and variously interpreting the text.

THE CONTEXT OF THE GITA

The Bhagavad-gita was spoken by Lord Krishna to his dear friend, Prince Arjuna, as they sat on a chariot between two armies eager for conflict. As the troops were making their final preparations, the blind Dhritarashtra was sitting in his palace in the capital, Hastinapura, worried as to how the proposed battle-site might favor his son's adversaries, the pious Pandavas. Even then, Kurukshetra was a famous pilgrimage site. Perturbed by these omens, Dhritarashtra confided in Sanjay, his personal secretary. Possessed of rare mystic vision, Sanjay saw within his heart events unfolding at Kurukshetra. In real time, he narrated to the blind monarch the entire Bhagavad-gita.

The Gita opens with Dhritarashtra's covert enquiry about the outcome of the battle. The king was subsequently encouraged to hear of Arjuna's hesitancy to fight, having seen friends, relatives and teachers on the opposite side. Dhritarashtra was positively elated when Arjuna, letting slip his fabled bow, refused to fight.

Overcome with despondency, Arjuna implored Krishna to become his mentor. Lord Krishna gladly explained how Arjuna's affection for his kinsmen was based on false compassion due to identification with the body. So illusioned, Arjuna viewed those connected with his physical body to be his kinsmen. In the first six chapters, Krishna explains how the real self (atman) is different from matter and can be elevated to self-realization through various types of yoga. During the second six chapters, he explores the Supreme, his service and his devotees. In the third and final six chapters, Krishna explains about the soul's entanglement with matter and how it achieves final liberation.

Inspired by these instructions, Arjuna lifted his bow, determined to fight. In the book's final verse, Sanjaya dashed Dhritarashtra's hopes by concluding, 'Wherever there is Krishna, the Supreme Lord, and wherever there is Arjuna, the greatest archer, there will certainly be morality, extraordinary power, opulence and victory. That is my opinion.'

THE CONTENT OF THE GITA

The late-medieval commentator Madhusudana Sarsvati divided the Gita into three sections, each of six chapters. By his classification, the first six chapters deal with karma-yoga (the path of action), the middle six with bhakti-yoga (the path of devotion)

Left This statue at the holy site of Kurukshetra depicts Krishna instructing Arjuna on the chariot.

Above A 20th-century painting of Krishna's universal form, as revealed to Arjuna in the 11th chapter of the Gita.

and the last six with jnana-yoga (the path of knowledge). Some commentators claim this progression indicates the supremacy of knowledge. To counter this, devotional scholars have compared the Gita to a sandwich, with the all-important conclusion spread in the middle. The Gita appears less amenable to the ritualistic karma-yoga, though it supports action tempered with knowledge and devotion.

The Gita has five subjects; the first three, typical of all Vedanta, are the self, God and matter. To these are added two others, namely karma (activity) and kala (time). Although the sacred dialogue is essentially a Vedantic text, it has assimilated elements of the other Darshanas, especially Yoga and Sankhya. Though not totally dismissive of the veneration of lesser deities, it is critical of pragmatic polytheism, the worship of specific deities for corresponding personal gains. It is less clear as to whether its proposed Supreme Deity is ultimately personal or impersonal.

The final six chapters provide many references to the Sankhya notion of three gunas (material qualities), providing a theological basis for evaluating ethical issues, as an alternative to texts dealing exclusively with dharma and morality, such as the more dated Manu Smriti. Though a few traditions grant the Gita scant authority, many accept it as a comprehensive guide to Hindu philosophy.

Below Krishna and Arjuna prepare for battle in this illuminated Bhagavad-gita produced in India over 200 years ago.

ARJUNA'S MORAL DILEMMA

Just before the battle, Arjuna faced a moral dilemma. He could regain his rightful kingdom only through fighting, and most likely killing, his friends and relatives. However, he anticipated that without his kinsmen's company, his kingdom would prove a hollow and fruitless victory.

His confusion epitomizes the ambivalence experienced by humans, who desire enjoyment but also foresee suffering for themselves and others. They resolve such tensions in two main ways: by subjugation of selfish desire or by indulgent abandonment. The former leads to upliftment and liberation, the latter to degradation and, in animal life, a temporary respite from the weight of moral responsibility. The unique human dilemma is expressed succinctly in the proverb, 'Two living beings are happy; the pig and the paramahamsa ('swan-like saint')'.

THE PURANAS AND OTHER TEXTS

ALTHOUGH HINDU TEXTS DISCUSS PHILOSOPHY, THEY ALSO REGULATE CONDUCT. THEY EXPLORE SOCIAL AND PERSONAL MORALITY AND PRESCRIBE VARIOUS MODES OF SADHANA (SPIRITUAL PRACTICE).

Narrative is important in providing examples of how Hindu ideals are expressed in everyday life and in making moral choices. Besides the two epics, most stories are found within the Puranas, which remain an important source of popular Hinduism.

THE PURANAS

Purana means 'ancient', and the books themselves claim greater antiquity than the Vedas. Scholars consider them more recent, going back to the time of the Gupta Empire between the 3rd and 5th centuries CE. Attributed to sage Vyasa, they describe the later deities, especially the Trimurti and their

Below Many stories tell of the conflict between the gods and demons. Here, in a rare moment of co-operation, they churn the ocean of milk.

respective consorts. There are 18 *maha* ('great') Puranas; three clusters of six, dedicated respectively to Brahma, Vishnu and Shiva. They extol the virtues of their favoured deity and theological concepts relevant to the corresponding community. There are also 18 'upa' or subsidiary Puranas. In South India, four Tamil Puranas glorify Lord Shiva who incarnated to teach the four boy-saints called the Kumaras.

The Puranas include accounts of creation, descriptions of stratified worlds, genealogies of deities and patriarchs, practical rules for living, and many popular myths and stories. They have been retold many times, taking the form of 'stories within a story'. Today, some of them are recited publicly at events called 'kathas'. Widely retold are the Bhagavata and Devi-Bhagavata Puranas, which include the famous

Above Tales of the child Krishna, such as his stealing butter – as shown here – are perhaps the most popular Puranic stories.

story of the goddess Durga killing the buffalo demon. Perhaps most popular is the Bhagavata Purana, which glorifies Lord Vishnu and 22 of his incarnations. It includes the much-loved stories of Lord Krishna.

THE DHARMA SHASTRAS

The Dharma Shastras include the law codes of Hinduism, which deal with three main subjects; codes of conduct, civil and criminal law, and punishment and atonement. Most important is the Manu Smriti, which is still consulted by the Indian legislature. It was written by Manu, the 'ruler of mankind' and the first law-giver. The word 'man' is said to derive from the title 'Manu', and there are 14 Manus during each universal creation. The Manu Smriti, containing 2,700 verses divided into 12 chapters, was probably written between 300 and 600 BCE.

Other important dharma texts were written by the sages Narada, Parashara and Yajnavalkya. Some Hindus now consider these texts dated, for they seem relevant only within the ancient Indian social context. In exploring contemporary ethical issues, modern Hindus often refer to texts like the Bhagavad-gita,

attempting to grasp the essence of moral principles rather than their literal application.

Another set of moral texts is the Artha Shastra, which explores the acquisition of wealth and power. One such popular work is by Chanakya, also known as Kautilya. As the prime-minister of King Chandragupta, he apparently helped the king defeat the Nandas, repulse Alexander the Great and establish the Mauryan Empire. Chanakya meticulously studied scripture to compile an anthology of popular wisdom (Niti-shastra) in the form of proverbs. The broad category of Niti-shastra also includes the famous fables of the Panchatantra and the Hitopadesha. Rather like Aesop's fables, they attribute specific characteristics to animals, such as nobility, foolishness or cunning. It is largely up to the reader to identify the moral of each story.

THE AGAMAS AND SECTARIAN LITERATURE

The Agamas do not derive their authority directly from the Vedas, but have been assimilated into the Vedic canon. They are also found within Jain and Buddhist traditions.

Left A modern painting of a tale called The Blue Jackal, *from the Panchatantra.*

Above A Mandi school painting, dated 1775, depicts the Puranic story of Durga slaying the buffalo demon.

In Hinduism, they form an enormous collection of Sanskrit scripture, often going by other names, such as Tantras and Samhitas. The Vaishnava Agamas feature two main sections, the Pancharatra Samhita and Vaikhanasas Samhita, which regulate all aspects of temple puja (worship). The Shaiva Agamas are more explicitly canonical texts and often considered Shruti by the Shaiva Siddhanta and Kashmiri Shaiva lineages. For Shaktas, there are 27 main Agamas, often called 'Tantras', usually taking the form of dialogue between Parvati and Shiva. All these texts expand on central theological teachings, usually in manner relevant to, or biased toward, the associated denomination.

Besides the Agamas, there are many other sectarian texts, central to one lineage but largely unknown to others. They usually derive legitimacy from the Vedic canon, taking the form of commentaries or summaries, often in vernacular languages. They also include hagiographies, the biographies of key saints and founders. Most sectarian texts are accommodated under Smriti, but may be considered revealed Shruti, equal in authority to the Vedas. While these two classifications are widely accepted, the precise status of any text and the dating of the work are often controversial. Hindus themselves have generally been uninterested in precise dating, considering the spirit and purpose of the books more important.

CHAPTER 3

HINDU TEACHINGS

Much Western intellectual history has been marked by tensions between the Church and the academic. In contrast, Hinduism has largely managed to reconcile faith and reason. Its philosophy is pragmatic, aimed at human liberation. Its religious commitment is philosophical, granting little credibility to mere conformity of belief. It strives to balance ambivalent views, and has little rejected its parent traditions, but instead adapted and assimilated them into progressively refined modes of understanding.

Hindu wisdom has been specifically perpetuated through lineages of gurus and their disciplines. In addition to its scholarly 'high' traditions, Hinduism features popular and village practices, based largely on meeting everyday needs. In all spheres, there are differences between the ideals of 'textual' Hinduism and the realities of daily practice.

Despite diversity of thought, Hinduism displays recurring themes, such as belief in a transmigrating self. Exploring the core notion of dharma (duty), texts list many human virtues, and examine morality through story and in relation to the Supreme. In discussing the nature and identity of God, Hinduism displays both bewildering diversity and great sophistication.

Opposite A contemporary painting depicting transmigration of the eternal self, a widely accepted concept that underpins much Hindu thought.

Above *On the banks of the River Ganges, a Hindu guru delivers a Pravachan, a religious and philosophical talk on scriptures.*

THE ETERNAL SELF

MODERN HINDU TEACHINGS USUALLY BEGIN WITH EXPLORING NOT
GOD BUT THE INDIVIDUAL SELF. THE SANSKRIT WORD FOR SELF IS
ATMAN, WHICH ULTIMATELY REFERS TO THE ETERNAL SOUL.

Hindu theology largely revolves around three main 'truths', namely the self, God and matter. Exploration of the relationships between these three generates further distinctive concepts. These notions lend some unity to Hinduism's diverse branches. However, in discussing the nature and identity of God, there is considerable diversity of opinion, with key debates focusing on the precise relationship between the self and the Supreme.

BRAHMAN

In Vedic times, the Supreme was called Brahman, the absolute and eternal reality. The Upanishads

Below Swami Tanmayananda Sarasvati performs meditation in his simple dwelling near Hampi, northern India. Traditionally, yoga, meditation and other spiritual practices aimed at realization of the practitioner's true, eternal identity.

and Vedanta philosophy describe Brahman as the all-pervading spirit. It is the source of the material creation, its support and its final resting place. Brahman has been identified with the individual self and with God, differentiating these two 'truths' from matter. However, it is imprecise to translate Brahman as 'God'. More accurately, Brahman refers to spirit, the eternal, conscious absolute standing in contrast to the relative and transient world of matter.

THE ATMAN

Hindu knowledge is largely intuitive and experiential, rather than theoretical or credal. Insight into Brahman (spirit) begins with contemplation on the nature of the self, as implied by the Upanishads, which declare 'That you are!' Similarly, Krishna begins his instructions in the Bhagavad-gita by discerning the self from the body. He states, 'Never was there a time I did not exist, nor

Above A Hindu bride gives the namaste greeting, which acknowledges the presence of the eternal in all others.

you, nor all these kings; nor in the future, shall any of us cease to be.' Krishna then explains that humans experience the self as unchanging throughout life, despite a constantly transmuting body. Consistent with Vedanta philosophy, he refutes the idea that consciousness emerges from matter, or that transient combinations produce an enduring self. Although material objects appear to

MATTER AND SPIRIT
Although the Vedas assert that 'everything is Brahman' (spirit), Brahman is initially differentiated from matter by its different characteristics, as shown below:

The self (spirit)	The body (matter)
Never-changing	Ever-changing
Eternal	Temporary
Conscious	Unconscious
Active	Inert
Alive	Dead

HINDU PHILOSOPHY

The notion of the eternal self is one of a number of concepts shared by most Hindu groups, and it greatly informs its various rituals and practices. Below is a concise overview of Hindu thought:

Almost all Hindus believe that the real self (*atman*) is eternal, made of spirit (*brahman*). The soul may take on a temporary material covering (physical body) and, by identifying with matter (*prakriti*), is entrapped by illusion (*maya*). Impelled by lust, greed and anger, he endures the cycle of repeated birth and death (*samsara*). Each soul creates its unique destiny determined by the universal law of karma (action and reaction). Under the influence of eternal time and the three material *gunas* (qualities), he moves throughout the creation, sometimes reaching higher planets, sometimes moving in human society, and at other times descending into lower species. Human life gives the opportunity to achieve *moksha*, liberation from this perpetual cycle, through re-identifying with the eternal Supreme (Brahman). Hinduism accepts different paths toward this common goal (liberation though union with God). At the same time, it stresses adherence to universal principles through performance of one's specified duty (*dharma*), as revealed through authorized holy books and the authentic *guru* (spiritual mentor).

Above A modern artist attempts to show how the changeless soul inhabits successive bodies, even within a single lifetime.

endure for some time, factually they are constantly changing. Krishna therefore explains, 'Those who are seers of the truth have concluded that of the nonexistent (the material body) there is no endurance and of the eternal (the soul) there is no change.' Whereas Western dualistic philosophy discerns mind from matter, Hindu thought holds that spirit, Brahman, is different from both gross matter (the physical body) and subtler forms (such as the mind).

VARIOUS ANALOGIES

Hindu texts present not only arguments but also many analogies to explain the self. For example, the atman is compared to the driver of a vehicle. As a chariot or car cannot run without a driver, similarly, the body will not work without the presence of the soul. The driver may tend to identify with his vehicle and feel kinship with drivers of a similar make and model. Similarly, feelings of friendship or enmity arise from identification with the body. By such identification, the driver also feels happiness or distress on account of the condition of the vehicle. In the event of an accident he may even cry out, 'You hit me!'

Hindu texts list further analogies. The mind and body are compared to layers of clothes worn by the self. To explain how the self becomes conditioned by matter, and yet does not change, they compare it to a diamond obscured by mud.

THE CYCLE OF BIRTH AND DEATH

ACCORDING TO HINDU THOUGHT, BECAUSE THE REAL SELF (ATMAN) IS UNCHANGING, IT SURVIVES DEATH. IN THIS WORLD, IT CONTINUOUSLY REINCARNATES, PASSING FROM ONE BODY TO THE NEXT.

The Bhagavad-gita explains: 'As the embodied soul continually passes in this body from boyhood to youth to old age, the soul similarly passes into a new body at death.' Through this process, called reincarnation, the self is carried within the subtle, astral body to its next destination. The precise nature of the new body is determined by the state of mind at death, and the mental impressions accumulated throughout life. The soul's destination is specifically influenced by two factors: the soul's desires and its accumulated merit (karma).

THE WORLD OF SAMSARA

Samsara broadly refers to this transient world and specifically to the cycle of repeated birth and death. Hindus consider consciousness to be present in all forms of life. Its potential is smothered, or conversely exhibited, to different degrees. Aquatics and plants are most covered, almost unconscious. Humans are most alert and spiritually awake. Souls, with their various levels of awareness, are accommodated within six hierarchical categories of life. They are, in order: aquatics; plants; insects and reptiles; birds; animals; and humans, including the residents of heaven. Most Hindus consider embodied life a painful cycle of four recurring problems: birth, disease, old age and death.

HEAVEN AND HELL

Explicit teachings on reincarnation date back to the Upanishads, and more rudimentary ideas informed the Vedic sacrifices, which elevated the performer to Indra's heaven.

Above In Kolkata, a mother protects her sleeping baby. For Hindu parents, the person within the new, infant body has arrived from elsewhere.

Today, dutiful sons still observe post-funeral rights, helping parents attain pitri-loka, 'the world of the ancestors' or other desirable destinations. The rites also prevent the departed soul from loitering as a ghost, or otherwise experiencing grief. The Sanskrit word for son, putra, means 'one who delivers from hell'. Although hell is largely associated with the lower species, the Puranas describe specific hellish worlds, overseen by the Lord of Death, Yama. However, residence in such 'hells' is usually considered temporary; so also the sojourn within Indra's heaven. Later teachings promoted an eternal paradise from which the self never returns. Contrary to traditional teachings, some contemporary gurus refute the idea of falling from human life into animal species.

A REINCARNATION STORY

King Bharata was such a pious and powerful king that India and Bharat are equally official short names for the Republic of India. As was then customary, he finally renounced the world, leaving the throne to the eldest of his 100 sons. After retiring to the

Left The Hindu funeral, like this one in Kanchipuram, marks the close of only one chapter of life.

OLD CLOTHES

The Bhagavad-gita compares the body to a set of clothes, which are replaced once they become old. As a person buys clothes on the basis of personal taste and available funds, the soul similarly obtains its next body according to its desires and its karmic credits. As a person wears layers of clothes, the soul is sheathed with layers of material coverings. They are primarily two: the subtle or astral body (lingam sharira), which continuously changes and accompanies the self at death, and the physical body, which is relinquished.

forest for austerity and meditation, he developed all saintly qualities, becoming gentle, soft-hearted and compassionate. One day, he rescued a baby deer from a raging river, and took it to his hermitage. There he fed the doe daily with fresh green grass and made sure it was comfortable. He lay down with it, bathed with it and even ate with it. When Bharata went to the forest to collect fruits and roots he would take the deer with him for fear that dogs, jackals or tigers might attack it. He enjoyed watching the deer leap, gambol and frolic like a child, and with great affection would carry it on his shoulders. However, as Bharata's heart filled with love for his pet, his inclination for spiritual practice drained away. Distracted from the path of self-realization and his meditation upon the Supreme, he thought of nothing but the delicate and innocent deer.

He was therefore mortified when, one morning, he found it absent from his side. In desperation, he searched everywhere. Wandering far from his ashram, he eventually

Right King Bharata died thinking of his pet fawn, and so entered a deer's body in his next life.

slipped from a cliff to his premature death. Thinking of the deer, he took a similar body in his next life. Because of his spiritual merit, his memory remained intact and, as a deer, he kept company with the saints in the forest. In the subsequent life, he was born as a great sage called Jada Bharata ('Stone-like Bharata'). To avoid further distraction from his spiritual quest, he ignored the world

Above A contemporary Hindu diorama depicts the self's transmigration through all stages of life.

and looked like a madman, unmindful of heat and cold, hunger and thirst or honour and dishonour. Internally, however, he always remembered God and, at death, finally attained release from the cycle of birth and death.

THE LAW OF KARMA

HINDU IDEAS ON REINCARNATION ARE CLOSELY LINKED TO NOTIONS
OF KARMA, A TERM THAT HAS NOW ENTERED THE ENGLISH LANGUAGE.
IT REFERS TO THE LAW OF UNIVERSAL ACCOUNTABILITY.

The Sanskrit term karma literally means 'action', but often refers to the corresponding reactions, or to the accumulated stock of such reactions. Thus, Hindus talk of 'good karma' and 'bad karma', the stored reactions that gradually fructify to reveal the soul's unique destiny.

Below Hindu children pet a young cow at the Pashupati temple on Kathmandu. Non-violence is based on empathy and an understanding of karma.

The accountability of the individual soul rests on its capacity for free will. Choice is exercised only in human form, for in passing through lower species the atman is bound by instinct and takes no moral decisions. Karma takes two main forms, namely punya (pious activities) and papa (impious activities). The Bhagavad-gita talks about a third type of action, akarma, which bestows neither good nor bad results, but grants liberation.

Above A modern, graphic depiction of the law of karma, from a tradition teaching strict vegetarianism.

GOOD AND BAD KARMA

Attaining a heavenly destination is compared to going on holiday. By pious conduct, the atman wins a celestial birth to enjoy without the toil of human existence. However, when the soul's pious credits are exhausted, he falls again to earth, just as the spent holidaymaker must return to the drudgery of work. With great facility for pleasure, the residents of heaven do not generally perform sinful actions, though texts abound with tales of celestials cursed to fall to earth for some indiscretion.

A lower birth is compared to confinement in prison. For transgressing universal laws, the self is degraded to the animal species. While there, the soul loses its exercise of free will and is condemned to a particular 'sentence'. Thereafter, through suffering, the atman is gradually purified and rises again to the human platform. Once more, the individual can choose to comply with nature's way or try to circumvent the law. The idea of karma is closely connected to the Vedic notion of rita (the natural order) and the later idea of dharma (prescribed duty). Karma is considered a natural and universal law, rather like the law of gravity.

THE SADHU'S BLESSINGS

A guru and his disciple were strolling through the city. By chance, they passed the crown prince of the kingdom mounting his fine white stallion. 'Greetings, holy man,' the prince called out. 'Please grant me your blessings.' Raising his palm, the sadhu replied, 'May you live forever.' As the prince gleefully cantered off, the sadhu explained, 'He now enjoys a life of unrestricted sense pleasure. However, when he dies he may suffer for his greed and licentiousness. It's best he lives forever.'

Later, they passed a celibate student collecting alms for his teacher. Seeing the sadhu, he placed his palms together and offered respect. The sadhu responded, 'May you die immediately.' The disciple queried, 'Master, why did you curse him to die?' The sadhu chuckled. 'That was a blessing. If he continues to live, his future is uncertain. At present, he is pure and sinless,

having performed many austerities. If he dies right now, he will attain the higher worlds.'

As they approached the market place, a ruddy-faced butcher called out to the sadhu, 'Morning! Any blessings for me today?' Raising his palm, the guru replied, 'May you neither live nor

Left A guru teaches his disciples about karma and personal accountability.

die.' The butcher scratched his head, muttering, 'What a strange blessing!' Turning to his equally perplexed disciple, the guru explained, 'The butcher's life is now hellish. And, for killing whimsically, without regulation, he will be born as an animal for thousands of lives. Whether he lives or dies, he will suffer.'

Next, they passed a temple where a devotee was praying to God. She did not even notice the sadhu approaching, but he called out, 'May you live or may you die.' 'Let me guess,' ventured the disciple, 'by remembering God, a devotee is always happy and free from karma. It makes no difference whether she lives or dies, for she will continue serving God in this life and in the next.' Smiling, the sadhu replied, 'My disciple, you are learning well.'

FREE WILL AND DESTINY

Karma suggests that each individual creates a unique destiny: therefore, fate can be changed. Most generally, this means that the individual may not necessarily avoid what is destined, but can choose a suitable response. Through the exercise of free will and choice, destiny for humans is in a constant state of flux. However, should the self fall from human form, free will is suspended and he must pass mechanically through the animal species.

There is wide debate about how karma can be nullified, as through penance, astrological remedy and surrender to God. Some schools of thought have developed sophisticated theologies, listing four types of karmic reaction which include the impetus to repeat the action, potentially initiating a chain of habitual behaviour. Particularly within village Hinduism, notions of karma are linked to belief in the power of curses, blessings and the evil eye. There are also debates about transference of karma, though most schools teach that the individual is ultimately responsible for his or her actions. The self cannot legitimately lay blame at the feet of others, including God.

Right Devotees immerse deities in the Yamuna River alongside foam from chemicals. In the modern world, karma is relevant to environmental issues.

MATTER

MATTER REFERS TO NON-CONSCIOUS ELEMENTS OF CREATION, WHICH CONSTITUTE INERT OBJECTS AS WELL AS THE MIND AND BODY. MATTER OPERATES ACCORDING TO THREE GUNAS (QUALITIES).

Most Hindu thought discerns spirit (Brahman) from matter (prakriti). Sankhya philosophy analyses prakriti and calls spirit the purusha (the enjoyer). In tantra, this dualism is represented as Shiva, the supreme male, and Shakti, representing matter. Modern Vedanta philosophy has assimilated the twin concepts of spirit and matter.

THE THREE GUNAS
Unlike spirit, matter is transient and undergoes the three stages of creation, maintenance and destruction. According to the Sankhya view, these phases correspond to three material qualities. The Sanskrit term is 'guna'. The three gunas are: goodness (sattva), which sustains; passion

Below Coloured powders sold during Holi festivities. As three primary colours can produce innumerable hues, so the three gunas, mixed in different proportions, fashion all species of life.

(rajas), which creates; and ignorance (tamas), which destroys. The gunas and their respective functions correspond to the three main deities; Brahma the creator, Vishnu the maintainer and Shiva the destroyer. The Bhagavad-gita explains how all material phenomena, including human conduct, can be analysed in terms of the gunas.

THE GUNAS AND COLOURS
The three gunas are represented as three colours. The purity of sattva is represented by yellow. The fiery nature of passion is symbolized by red. The darkness of ignorance is denoted by dark blue. The metaphor of three colours further explains the gunas. As from just the three primary colours a whole palette can be created, so combinations of the three gunas generate the entire range of life forms. They fall into three main categories. Human society, living in the middle planetary systems, is

Above Each guna is identified with one of the Trimurti (three main deities). The Trimurti once descended as a single avatar called Dattatreya, shown here.

propelled mainly by passion. The residents of the celestial realms are guided by goodness. The animal species submit to the tight grip of ignorance. Therefore, by developing the virtues of sattva, humans may be elevated; conversely, contamination with tamas binds the self and propels it into the lower species. Even within human society, predominated by passion, mixtures of the gunas create diversity and various psychophysical characteristics.

RELATED PRACTICES
The guna-model is used to classify human conduct. In modern Hinduism, it is useful in determining moral responses and lifestyle choices. Sattva represents desirable conduct; passion is acceptable; and ignorance is to be avoided. At the same time, all three are important, since even the functions of ignorance, such as sleep, are essential to life. The Bhagavad-gita also teaches that the original system of four

varnas was based not on birth, but on guna and karma: the person's qualities and disposition toward a particular type of work. Although the quality of goodness, and related social functions such as education, are deemed most desirable, all elements of society are essential.

Similarly, although animals are under the sway of ignorance, they should be treated kindly. Their exhibition of consciousness, however faint, suggests the presence of the atman. In Hindu texts, knowledge is defined not as facts or information but as values. Most important is human empathy. A lack of sensitivity toward other people and all living creatures is a primary symptom of ignorance. Many Hindus therefore regard the process of transmigration as a means by which the eternal self learns by experience; for example, a person unkind to animals may be awarded such a body. Some traditions list three specific bodies the self takes immediately before ascending again to human life; they are the contented cow, which symbolizes goodness; the lion, which represents the royal quality of passion; and the mischievous monkey, which represents ignorance.

Below Each of the gunas is represented by an animal that reflects its characteristics.

SATTVA (GOODNESS)	RAJAS (PASSION)	TAMAS (IGNORANCE)

Sustainability (Vishnu)	Creativity (Brahma)	Destruction (Shiva)
Serenity, contentment, knowledge, purity, seeing things clearly, honesty, self-control and magnanimity	Desire, ambition, action, attachment, intense endeavour and the desire to enjoy and control	Inertia, hopelessness, darkness, intoxication, madness, excessive sleep and refusal to consider consequences
Results in wisdom	Results in greed	Results in illusion/madness
Qualities of a qualified Brahmin according to system of four varnas	Qualities of the Kshatriya (mixed with sattva) and Vaishya (mixed with tamas)	Qualities strong in the Shudra class, those employed by others
At death, elevated to higher, heavenly planets	Reincarnates again as a human on earth	Enters lower species or lower planets at death
Knowledgeable, seeing all living beings as equal, with concern for their wellbeing	Discriminates between different people and various creatures	Unaware of, or ignores, the feelings and suffering of other living beings
Food is balanced, healthy and tasty; promotes longevity	Food is too rich, sweet, hot etc., and taken just for pleasure	Food is old, unhealthy or unhygienic, made by violence or fermentation
Acting like this is painful at first but gives long-term joy	Gives immediate pleasure, but regret in the long-tern	Acting like this gives no happiness, now or later
One knows what is right and what is wrong	One is unsure about what is right and wrong	One is convinced right is wrong and vice versa
One is alert and fixed on the present moment	One hankers, and looks to the future	One is debilitated by lamentation and lack of hope
Works smartly and dutifully without excessive effort	Works very hard, desirous of enjoying the fruits	Avoids work; lazy, inactive and prone to sleep

MOKSHA: LIBERATION FROM BIRTH AND DEATH

MOST TRADITIONS AGREE THAT LIBERATION IS THE ULTIMATE GOAL OF HUMAN LIFE. THE MAIN DIFFERENCES FOCUS ON TWO ISSUES: FIRST, THE MEANS OF ACHIEVING MOKSHA; SECOND, ITS PRECISE NATURE.

The Advaita traditions teach that moksha is achieved through knowledge and the realization that the individual soul is identical to an impersonal God. The dualistic traditions claim that the atomic self remains ever distinct from a personal Supreme and that liberation depends on devotion, self-surrender and the grace of both God and guru.

MONISTIC PHILOSOPHY

In Advaita philosophy, the soul is compared to a drop of water, which, with liberation, merges into the vast ocean representing the Supreme. A further analogy is that of the water pot, which has both inside and outside. Once the pot is broken, the two

Below Burning ghats besides the Ganges in the holy city of Varanasi. Hindus believe that dying here hastens liberation for the departed soul.

immediately disappear. Similarly, while the soul is embodied it perceives itself to be limited, but upon liberation realizes its identity as the all-pervading Supreme. Hence, for the Advaita schools, the soul and God are identical in every respect. Liberation entails realization of one's Godhood as the atman merges into Brahman, the all-pervading consciousness, or, some say, realizes that it never was separated.

DUALISTIC PHILOSOPHIES

Other schools have compared liberation to a green bird entering a tree. It appears to have 'merged', but actually the bird (the self) retains its separate identity from the tree (God). Although the soul realizes its identity as Brahman (spirit), different from the perishable mind and body, it remains an individual, distinct from God and other souls.

Above For some Hindus, liberation means merging with the supreme consciousness, as a water drop loses its individuality upon merging with the ocean.

In response to the pot analogy, dualists cite the example of clay, which can be moulded into different forms such as cups, bowls and plates. Similarity, both the individual soul and God, though of the same substance, exhibit different spiritual forms. Union for the personalist refers to a unity of purpose, through loving service. Liberation means returning to a spiritual world to engage in activities of loving exchange.

DEBATES ON LIBERATION

In early Vedic Hinduism, life's main aim was to reach a temporary heaven. Somewhat later, the Upanishads postulated an eternal world. Shankara viewed this as a vibrant impersonal energy called the brahmajyoti (Brahman effulgence). Ramanuja was the first to write of Vaikuntha, a complete paradise in which the liberated self is an eternal associate of Vishnu. Later schools delineated up to five different types of liberation, which include both Shankara's and Ramanuja's conceptions.

There has also been wide debate about the soul attaining liberation before death. Ramanuja and his followers consider it impossible. Most Advaitins and some personalists, like the Bengali Vaishnavas, deem

Above For some Hindus, the soul retains its individuality, despite perceived unity with God, as with this bird in a tree.

it possible and call the liberated soul a 'jivanmukta'; here, jiva is another term for soul, and mukti, an alternative for moksha, means liberated.

There are also widely different opinions as to the precise causes of liberation, variously posited as conduct, knowledge, detachment and devotion. Polemics also revolve around contrary stances on the respective roles of grace and personal endeavour. Some devotional schools advertise an aim of life above even liberation, namely prema (love of God). For them, God-infused saints even shun liberation, for they reside always in the spiritual realm even while apparently walking the earth.

GAJENDRA THE ELEPHANT

Though the following story is popular with the devotional schools, the great monist Shankara refers to it in his prayer called 'Eight prayers dedicated to Lord Krishna'. It indicates popular belief in the primacy of grace in achieving liberation.

A powerful king in South India retired from active life to meditate in the jungle. One day, the famous sage Agastya entered the hermitage, but the king, deep in meditation, failed to welcome him properly. The angry Agastya cursed the king to become a

dull elephant, and so the unfortunate monarch was reborn as Gajendra, king of the elephants. Naturally, he forgot all about his previous birth.

One hot day, accompanied by female elephants, he went to enjoy bathing in the crystal waters of a nearby lake. The water's inhabitants were disturbed and, in anger, the chief crocodile immediately seized Gajendra's leg with his powerful jaws. A great fight ensued, but within the water the elephant became weak, whereas the crocodile's power increased. Despite his considerable strength, Gajendra realized his helplessness, and in his desperation

remembered the mantras he had repeatedly recited in his previous life. Offering these prayers, he sought God's shelter. Vishnu immediately swept down, riding on the back of his giant eagle, Garuda. With his disk, he severed the head of the crocodile, whose soul immediately merged with the Lord's own effulgence. Gajendra was saved and, in a four-armed spiritual form, mounted the back of Garuda, who whisked him back to the spiritual world.

Below A poster of Vishnu flying down on Garuda to liberate the elephant Gajendra.

THREE ASPECTS OF GOD

HINDU TEXTS DESCRIBE THE ABSOLUTE REALITY AS SAT-CHIT-ANANDA: 'ETERNAL, CONSCIOUS AND BLISSFUL'. FOR MANY SCHOOLS, THESE QUALITIES CORRESPOND TO THREE PERSPECTIVES ON GOD.

Texts describe three aspects of the divine: first, Brahman, God existing everywhere; second, antaryami, God situated within the heart; and third, Bhagavan or Ishvara, God residing outside, beyond this world.

These three features are compared to the sun, the sunshine and the sun's reflection in pots of liquid. As heat and light, the all-pervading sunshine is qualitatively like the sun, yet the fiery and luminescent orb retains its separate form and identity. Furthermore, as that one sun is

Below According to Hindu thought, the air exists outside solid earth, but also within it. Similarly, the impersonal Supreme (Brahman) pervades everything.

reflected in numerous pots of water, the same God is reflected in the hearts of all living beings. Hindu denominations often favour one of these three aspects and dispute the relationships between them. The sun analogy is favoured by monotheists, who claim that the personal aspect of God, Bhagavan, is the source of both the impersonal Brahman and the Lord within.

GOD EVERYWHERE

Brahman refers to the all-pervading aspect of the absolute. Since everything comes from the absolute, it is identical with it. The Upanishads state, 'Everything is Brahman'. The same texts relate the story of Svetaketu, whose teacher instructs

Above A painting showing a yogi meditating on the antaryami, God's form within his heart.

him to dissolve salt in a tumbler of water. Asked if he sees the salt, the boy replies 'no'. However, when his teacher asks him to sip the water repeatedly, after each sip pouring

some away, Svatakeu affirms that each time he can taste the salt. The lesson is that Brahman, despite being invisible, pervades the entire universe.

This sat or eternal aspect of God is initially perceived by apprehending the eternal nature of the self. This insight is the foundation for much Hindu thought and forms Krishna's first instruction in the Bhagavad-gita. According to the impersonal school, this realization is complete when one apprehends oneself as the all-pervading Supreme. For monotheistic schools, Brahman realization is but a preliminary phase of knowledge.

GOD WITHIN THE HEART

Antaryami, means 'the controller within' and refers to God within the hearts of all living beings, and within each atom. By this means, the Supreme is omniscient and it represents his chit (knowing) aspect. According to the Puranas, the Antaryami is initially perceived in three ways. In matter, he is reflected in the awesome features of nature; in the lower species, he is revealed as instinct; and in humans, he is perceived as memory, intelligence, inspiration, conscience and exceptional ability. He is the object of meditation for many mystic yogis. The Katha Upanishad likens the atman and the Antaryami to two birds sitting within the tree of the heart.

GOD AS A PERSON

Ishvara means 'lord', and indicates God, or a particular god or goddess, situated outside oneself or beyond the world. The alternative term, Bhagavan, means 'one who possesses unlimited opulence'. Parashara Muni, father of the author Vyasa,

Right God or 'Bhagavan', here represented as Krishna, lives in his own world, way beyond the material creation.

SCRIPTURAL VERSES ON THE SUPREME

The following verses explain three aspects of God, which are compared to the sun's rays, the sun's reflections in as many pots of liquid, and the sun planet itself.

Above This painting shows the sun (God beyond), the sunshine (God everywhere), and the sun's numerous reflections in pots of liquid (God within).

'That Brahman is in front and at the back, in the north, east, south and west, and overhead and below. In other words, that supreme Brahman effulgence spreads throughout both the material and spiritual skies.'
Mundaka Upanishad

'The Lord is situated in everyone's heart, O Arjuna, and directs the wanderings of all living entities . . .'
Bhagavad-gita 18.61

'Bhagavan is he who possesses unlimited strength, fame, wealth, knowledge, beauty and renunciation.'
Vishnu Purana 7.60

---

has listed six categories of opulence: fame, wealth, strength, beauty, knowledge and renunciation. This feature of the absolute embodies both omnipotence and ananda (happiness).

Bhagavan refers to a person with whom the soul can have a direct relationship as a source of spiritual pleasure. For some scholars, and many bhakti traditions, all pleasure is essentially derived from relationships. The words Bhagavan and Ishvara quite closely resemble the English term 'God'. The word Brahman is a more philosophical term, better translated as 'spirit' or 'Absolute Reality'.

DIFFERENT SCHOOLS

Most traditions accommodate the three aspects of the divine, but understand them and their respective statuses differently. For the pure monist, the personified deity (Ishvara or Bhagavan) falls within the world of illusion, and deity worship is a means toward the higher realization of the impersonal Brahman. For many bhakti schools, with elements of dualism, the personal form of God as Bhagavan or Ishvara is the highest, and the impersonal Brahman is but God's effulgence. The mystic yogis, who initially perform hatha-yoga exercises, often meditate on the Antaryami, the lord within. The various religious orders also differ as to their precise understanding of the many gods and goddesses.

GOD WITH AND WITHOUT FORM

HINDUS ACCEPT GOD WITH AND WITHOUT FORM. DEBATE FOCUSES ON THE RELATIONSHIP BETWEEN THESE TWO FEATURES, THEIR RESPECTIVE STATUSES AND EXPLAINING THE MANY DEITIES.

Hinduism accommodates many concepts of God, including pantheism and polytheism. However, the high scholarly traditions emphasize the singularity of the Supreme, an idea that often underpins even village practices and the veneration of many gods and goddesses. Within

Below Some scholars consider the universe a form of God, as seen in this carving of Krishna at a temple in Guwahati.

modern Vedanta, there are two main doctrines: Advaita (monism) and Dvaita (dualism). Monism propounds an impersonal absolute. Dualism, sometimes also called monotheism, conversely teaches that God is intrinsically personal. The two corresponding features of God are called nirguna Brahman (the absolute without attributes) and saguna Brahman (the absolute with attributes). Generally speaking, the

Above A representation of God as the formless, all-pervading consciousness.

nirguna feature has no form and the saguna feature has form. The two main doctrines argue about which feature, if either, is higher.

ADVAITA (MONISM)

Advaita means 'non-dual' and refers to the doctrine of monism, by which the soul, God and matter constitute a homogenous whole. As Brahman, the soul and God are identical in all respects. This doctrine was most effectively propagated by Shankara (788–820CE), who taught that Brahman is ultimately nirguna, without form, activity and personality. The unperceivable and inconceivable Brahman is represented through personalized deities for the understanding and veneration of common people, who project their mundane experience of form on to the impersonal divine. These forms are therefore called 'anthropomorphic'. For Advaitins, God is ultimately nirguna. The saguna feature may be helpful but is ultimately imaginary and illusory.

DVAITA (DUALISM)

The dualistic schools teach that the soul and God are eternally distinct. Furthermore, God is saguna, exhibiting eternal form, activity and personhood. The view is theomorphic, holding that human form is shaped on God, and that this world reflects the prototypical spiritual realm.

Above The Indian monsoon refracts white light into seven colours. For many Hindus, the many deities represent the diverse attributes of the single impersonal Supreme.

For its inclusion of lesser gods and goddesses, this stance has been termed 'inclusive monotheism'.

The theological foundations for monotheism were laid down by Ramanuja, who qualified Shankara's uncompromising 'monism'. Like Ramanuja, most post-Shankara theologians accepted elements of Advaita. Only Madhva taught the antithesis, dualism, thus refuting any similarity between the soul and God. Strictly speaking, the word Dvaita refers to Madhva's teaching of 'pure dualism'. Most schools teaching dualism – in its broader sense – acknowledge nirguna Brahman, while also accepting, or even favouring, the personal, saguna feature.

EXPLAINING MANY DEITIES
The two broad schools differently explain the many devas (gods) and devis (goddesses). Monists consider all deities equal, with each representing a specific attribute of an impersonal God. They liken the

Right This temple mural in Dallas, Texas, depicts belief in a God who enjoys spiritual form and personal relationships.

deities to the colours of the rainbow, revealed as white light refracts though rain drops. When the one impersonal divine is distorted through this world, humans apprehend many deities.

The monotheistic stance likens God to the prime minister, the head of many government officers. Most deities are considered subordinate to the main Deity, and dependent for their power and authority. As citizens approach the government through a representative, similarly veneration of lesser gods is an indirect means of approaching God. The analogy conveys how God and his authority pervade the universe, while he retains his personal form, identity and residence.

THE MURTI
Of several other core notions related to God, two are paramount. First, the idea that God can 'expand' or duplicate himself into unlimited forms, without diminishing his original potency; second, the view that God can descend as an avatara ('one who comes down'). A key type of avatara is the murti, the sacred image, whose worship has historically met with much opposition and violence. However, sophisticated Hindu theologies imply that it is hasty to dismiss image worship as mere superstition or 'idol worship'.

Advaitins teach that the omniscient and omnipresent Brahman is unarguably present in the murti, which makes the inconceivable and

Above Former Indian prime minister Manmohan, surrounded by other ministers, reflects the idea of one Supreme Person assisted by many subservient deities.

unperceivable visible to human eyes. They often describe the murti as a meditational aid, and its worship may be discarded upon adopting the higher, difficult path of impersonal, nirguna worship.

For the personalist, and in much common practice, the murti is more that a 'container for the spirit'. It actually is the deity, fully conscious of the worshipper. Devotional schools teach that in order to receive and reciprocate the devotee's love, God or a specific deity appears in a form that is visible yet fully spiritual. For devotees, divine relationships are real, and the blueprint of mundane familial affairs. They can be intimate, devoid of fear and inordinate reverence. Out of love, God may even take an apparently inferior role, as a loyal servant, affectionate child or hen-pecked lover. There are many stories of the temple deities talking and reciprocating with their devotees, or even quitting the shrine. In one temple in the sacred town of Vrindavana, the altar curtains are swished open only momentarily in case Krishna again leaves to sport with his devotees.

SOURCES OF AUTHORITY

HINDU TEACHINGS ARE DERIVED FROM TWO MAIN SOURCES; THE FIRST, HINDU HOLY TEXTS, AND, THE SECOND, THE REALIZATIONS OF HOLY PEOPLE. A THIRD SOURCE OF AUTHORITY IS CONSCIENCE.

When a Hindu boy undergoes his sacred thread initiation, to become 'twice-born', he ritually accepts scripture as his spiritual mother and the guru (spiritual teacher) as his new father. A third authoritative voice, the Antaryami or 'guru within', acknowledges the need for reflection and a high degree of self-autonomy.

SCRIPTURE

Hindu groups are legitimized not by allegiance to a particular creed but by broad submission to the Vedic scriptural authority. However, such subscription is not whimsical, and requires an aspiring tradition to write insightful textual commentaries. Many sacred lineages also trace their origins to a particular deity,

Below In the holy town of Udupi is a golden statue of Vyasa dictating the Mahabharata to his scribe, Ganesha.

implying that God remains the fountainhead of all authority.

Hindu scripture is called shabda-brahman (spiritual sound), alluding to its oral transmission. Tradition teaches that texts were only written as human memory began to falter, around 3,000BCE. Shabda-brahman, or simply 'shabda', is often considered the most reliable form of authority for spiritual matters. When using other forms of evidence, such as empirical and rational knowledge, shabda remains the guiding standard. Many groups acknowledge that the flawed mind and senses are unable to extend human knowledge to the spiritual dimension. To re-awaken the self, an external source of knowledge is required. The Vedas are compared to the mother, who first gives knowledge. Theistic schools have explained how the mother most authentically reveals the identity of the father (God).

Above Treating sacred texts reverentially acknowledges their authoritative status with regard for spiritual knowledge.

GURU

The guru plays a central role in Hinduism, often serving as an intermediary between the soul and God. Many schools claim that divine guidance and benediction descend through the genuine spiritual teacher, who acts and speaks for God. Also on behalf of the divine, the guru accepts the disciple's service and veneration.

Accepting a true guru is essential for understanding and realising scripture. The Svetashvatara Upanishad (6.38) explains: 'Only unto to great souls who have unflinching faith in both the Lord and the guru, are all the imports of Vedic knowledge automatically revealed'. Realization without mentorship is often considered impossible, as the seeker is inevitably waylaid by *maya* (illusion or ignorance). A guru is required to understand and realize scripture.

There are debates about the guru's exact identity. Some traditions equate the guru with God, whereas others insist that he or she is God's representative. Whatever their opinion, many Hindus still accept initiation from a spiritual teacher, thus becoming formal disciples. Respect is also shown toward other

holy figures, such as brahmins and sadhus (monks); even to family elders, and to regular teachers, also called 'guru'.

THE GURU WITHIN
The notion of dharma does not demand blind obedience to duty. Arjuna is praised for displaying foresight and consideration before the battle of Kurukshetra. The entire Mahabharata explores moral dilemmas and the need to take decisions based on unique circumstances. For this, the role of the Antaryami, the 'Lord in the heart', is considered essential. However, acting on conscience is counterbalanced by the need to also reflect on scripture and the guru's instructions, and to assimilate their real meaning.

BLIND FOLLOWING
The following story from southern India illustrates the need to carefully discern the real mood and mission of the guru and, indeed, the actual meaning of scripture:

Guru Paramartha decided to go on pilgrimage. He ordered his five disciples to purchase a horse but, with few funds, they returned with an old, unsteady nag. Concerned, the guru informed his disciples that they should pick up anything that might fall from the horse.

At an auspicious hour, the sacred journey began. One day, a low branch brushed off Guru Paramartha's turban. An enthusiastic disciple ran back to retrieve it. As he ran forward again, he noted something else coming not off the horse but out of it. In a fit of inspiration, he used the turban to collect it and humbly offered the turban to his guru. Having re-donned his

Above A shrine near London depicts the five most recent members of a lineage of spiritual teachers.

head-piece, Guru Paramartha was somewhat upset, and loudly rebuked and berated his foolish disciple. His student was completely confused. Had he not sincerely followed his guru's orders?

'All right, all right!' conceded the holy man. 'Okay, take your notebook and write down these items. If any of *these* fall off, pick them up and return them to me. Otherwise, please leave them! Okay, here they are; turban, umbrella, water cup, meditation beads ...' And so the list went on. The disciple was happy, and Guru Paramartha anticipated no more dousing with horse manure.

However, on a stretch of treacherous road, the old nag slipped and tumbled. The enthusiastic disciple righted the horse and consulted his list. On to the animal's back he faithfully loaded his guru's turban, beads, water pot, Bhagavad-gita – in fact, everything – and joyfully proceeded, leaving his beloved guru writhing in the mud!

Left In New Zealand, a disciple worships a sacred image of his guru, considered the embodiment of spiritual wisdom.

SANATANA DHARMA

SANTANA DHARMA REFERS TO RELIGION UNBOUNDED BY A SPECIFIC 'FAITH', CREED, COUNTRY, ETHNICITY OR TIME PERIOD. FOLLOWERS CLAIM IT IS A TIMELESS, UNIVERSAL AND INCLUSIVE RELIGION.

Many Hindus call their own religion 'sanatana dharma'. Some scholars question the idea of 'an eternal religion', perhaps suspecting an attempt to deny change and cling to tradition. Hindu thinkers claim differently, that the term acknowledges the enduring nature of moral and spiritual laws, not dissimilar to physical axioms. The idea of universal, unchanging laws is linked to the Vedic notion of rita, 'the natural order'.

THE MEANING OF DHARMA

Hinduism later adopted the term 'dharma', 'the natural law'. Although popularly translated as 'duty' or 'religion', its more profound meaning is derived from the Sanskrit root 'dhri', which means 'to sustain'. A further connotation is 'that which is integral to an object'. Hence, the dharma of fire is to be hot, of sugar to be sweet. For humans, dharma consists of duties that sustain them according to their innate characteristics.

These human predispositions are twofold, spiritual and material, generating two equivalent sets of duty. The first, sanatana dharma, reflects a person's real identity as the eternal atman. Sanatana dharma nurtures the eternal relationship between the self and God. On the other hand, varnashrama-dharma takes account of the soul's psycho-physical situation, classifying duties according to four ashramas (stages in life) and four varnas (classes). However, since diversity is prevalent in any human society,

Above At the River Ganges, a holy man offers respects to the rising sun. As the sun is the same for all people, sanatana dharma teaches about shared religious truths.

varnashrama is sometimes identified with the eternal order, and considered part of the sanatana dharma.

DHARMA AS INCLUSIVE

A distinctive Hindu view is that 'God' refers to the absolute reality, not merely a human, social or evolutionary construct. Hence, Hindus rarely imply that God is the property of a particular ethnic or religious group. God is one despite variant beliefs. To explain this, gurus cite the analogy of the sun, which remains singular despite variant names in different tongues. The Divine similarly transcends temporary designations such as 'British' or 'Indian', 'Hindu', 'Jewish' or 'Muslim'. The real self (atman) is also beyond such labels. Hence religion, aiming at reunion with God, is above all sectarian designations.

To explain plural religious traditions, Hindu teachings employ another metaphor. They liken

Left Followers of sanatana dharma highlight its inclusive connotations. This statue of Lord Jesus Christ overlooks an ashram in Jeevan Dara, North India.

religion to knowledge, which is common to all, despite students attending different universities. As mathematical theorems are equally valid in Greece, India or Britain, so the topic of study is identical for all religious traditions. Favouring the idea of a shared, inclusive wisdom, Hinduism makes little use of the terms 'creed', 'belief' or 'faith'. Despite this most Hindus value fidelity to a particular religion, denomination or deity, rather than a whimsical, self-selective approach. Many inherit a kula-deva (family deity) and may select a particular ishta-deva (chosen deity) for their individual devotion.

SANATANA DHARMA IN PRACTICE

Many Hindus include members of other authorized religions under the banner of sanatana dharma, whilst retaining a preference for their own 'school'. For this reason, many avoid the word 'conversion', for it wrongly suggests that faith traditions are discrete and mutually exclusive. In practice, most Hindus don't restrict

Below Mumbai University teaches subjects similar to other modern universities. Hindu thought stresses the idea of shared knowledge, despite various institutions or 'faiths'.

temple attendance to a particular deity or denomination, and are happy to attend churches, gurudwaras and other places of worship.

However, Hinduism doesn't always meet its ideals. Medieval South India witnessed tension and violence between worshippers of Shiva and Vishnu. More recently, conversion attempts by Muslim and Christian communities, and strategies for re-conversion, have fuelled social tensions in Orissa and Kerala. Broader controversies rage about nationalism and the complex relationships between Hinduism and India. Most conspicuously, caste discrimination remains a blot on the inclusive Hindu landscape.

The medieval bhakti saints challenged the hereditary caste system. Some, such as Kabir, drew from other faiths such as Sufism and accepted followers irrespective of their class, gender or religious background. Devotional movements drew on the ideal of sanatana dharama to propagate theories of spiritual egalitarianism, asserting everyone's right to spiritual life and teaching that the inescapable disposition of the living entity (atman) is service (seva). In the 20th century, and especially outside

Above Some Hindus preach, such as this Argentinian member of the Hare Krishna movement selling books in Central Park, New York.

India, many temples called themselves 'sanatanist', indicating preference for an eclectic form of Hinduism without bias toward one specific denomination or lineage.

21st-century scholars have identified two broad ideologies competing for the loyalties of the Hindu community. One of these, Hindu nationalism, largely conflates Hinduism and Indian patriotism. The other, articulated by such figures as Mahatma Gandhi, represents Hinduism as the 'eternal' or 'universal' religion. However, the two ideas are often mixed, perhaps ambivalently, as when nationalists praise India as the sole source of a universal spirituality. On the other hand, for those who favour inclusivity, there are difficult questions as to how far Hinduism should resist aggression. Despite different responses to these issues, the concept of sanatana dharma challenges a narrow understanding of 'religion' and, for Hindus themselves, remains a core ideal.

VARNASHRAMA DHARMA

VARNASHRAMA DHARMA REFERS TO THE ORIGINAL HINDU SOCIAL SYSTEM, WITH DUTIES BASED ON THE CITIZEN'S POSITION IN A PARTICULAR VARNA (SOCIAL CLASS) AND ASHRAMA (STAGE OF LIFE).

According to Hindu texts, varnashrama refers to natural classifications apparent in all societies. The four varnas (classes) take account of different predispositions towards work and the required qualifications. The four ashramas mirror natural phases in life, during which certain duties are conducive to wellbeing. Hindu texts imply that individuals realize their potential by respecting such natural laws, and that society should be organized hierarchically.

Right A diagrammatic representation of the four varnas and their respective relationships with the entire social body.

SPECIFIC DUTIES

The Rig Veda compares the social body to the human form. In that metaphorical body, the priestly and academic *brahmanas* are the head; the kshatriyas (warriors) are the arms; the *vaishyas* (business community) are the thighs and belly; and the *shudra* working class are the legs. The analogy gives insight into the respective

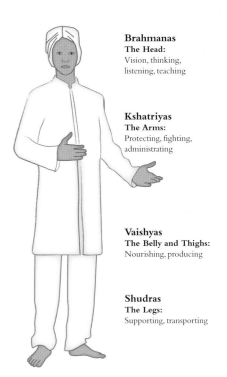

Brahmanas
The Head:
Vision, thinking, listening, teaching

Kshatriyas
The Arms:
Protecting, fighting, administrating

Vaishyas
The Belly and Thighs:
Nourishing, producing

Shudras
The Legs:
Supporting, transporting

WOMEN'S DUTIES

Although women are classified by varna, they have long been considered a section of society in their own right. Women do not pass through the four stages available to men, but through three phases, described in the text called the Manu Smriti:

1 As a child protected by her father
Traditionally, girls did not receive a formal academic education. Women's role was considered essential in preserving social and cultural values, learned mainly at home.

2 As a wife, protected by her husband
Hinduism places great value on pre-marital chastity and this has greatly influenced domestic customs. Girls were betrothed and married at a young age. In married life, the wife's role was centred on the home and she was not concerned with earning family income. Responsibilities as a loving and available parent were considered paramount.

3 As an elder or widow, protected by the eldest son
If the husband died, took sannyasa or became an invalid, the eldest son would maintain her. In respectable families, elders were treated with respect and their opinions sought on key family issues.

In the modern liberal context, the very notion of 'protection' has often been interpreted to suggest exploitation. Although protecting women has remained a core Hindu ideal, reality

Above A family prays at their household shrine. The term 'ashrama' suggests all life stages are 'places of spiritual culture'.

has fallen short. Single women and new brides have been exploited to secure dowries, and widows not only unsupported, but also forced from home to live in ashrams. It remains debatable how much such abuse has been spawned by religious teachings, or conversely by greed, poverty and social anomaly.

Right A modern painting of the four varnas, which represent personal dispositions as well as social classes.

social functions. The brahmanas are responsible for vision, represented by the eyes, and for teaching, symbolized by the mouth. The kshatriya's main duty is to protect society, as the arms do for the body. The main concern of the vaishya (business-community) is material nourishment, and those employed by others, the shudras, support other sections of society. The same metaphor is sometimes used to explain the four ashramas, which are, from the feet up, student life, marriage, retirement and renunciation.

Each varna and ashrama has its own specified dharma. What is desirable for one section of society may be detrimental to another. For example, serenity and contentment are vital to the priestly varna but disastrous to the warrior class. Contact with money and women is essential for householders, but spiritually suicidal for the celibate renunciant. Underlying these social differences are the shared notions of mutual service and incremental spiritual progress.

VARNASHRAMA AND CASTE

The social system called varnashrama is controversial due to its association with modern caste practices. Many Hindus distance themselves from varnashrama, considering it a mere sociological phenomenon or an outdated religious practice. Others accept the four ashramas but reject the four varnas. Most common among Hindu scholars is the view that modern, hereditary caste practice is a perversion of the original varnashrama system. The two are not necessarily synonymous. Mahatma Gandhi, the most famous critic of caste abuse, believed in the original principles of varnashrama dharma. The system of four varnas was apparently based on mutual support and service, allowing for upward and downward mobility. The caste system, as it evolved, became rigid and hereditary, motivated by a desire to artificially maintain privilege and the status quo.

THE FOUR VARNAS • Brahmins – priests, teachers and intellectuals • Kshatriyas – armed forces, police and government •Vaishyas – farmers, business and trades-people • Shudras – artists, craftsmen and workers	**THE FOUR ASHRAMAS** • Brahmachari ashrama – celibate student life • Grihastha ashrama – householder life •Vanaprastha ashrama – retired life • Sannyasa ashrama – renounced life *Right Vaishnava sannyasis, members of the fourth ashrama, at Ujjain.*

ONE GOAL, DIFFERENT PATHS

HINDUISM DOES NOT PRESCRIBE ONE PATH FOR ALL. BASED ON INDIVIDUAL DISPOSITION, IT OFFERS DIVERSE INCENTIVES TOWARD LIBERATION AND DIFFERENT PATHS TOWARD ULTIMATE SUCCESS.

Hinduism makes little distinction between sacred and secular, or between religious and worldly duties. Culture and religion have also been closely intertwined. Hence, religious practice accommodates both material and spiritual goals.

FOUR GOALS

Hindu texts list four sequential aims: dharma, artha, kama and moksha. Dharma (righteous living) facilitates artha (the acquisition of wealth). Economic stability enables humans to enjoy regulated kama (sensual pleasure). Finally, the futility of flickering gratification promotes a search for a permanent solution to life's problems, through

Below Jain temple on the holy Mount Girnar, Gujarat. Many Hindus compare the different yogas to equally valid paths up the same mountain.

moksha (salvation). Later lineages, considering the desire for liberation to be self-centred, have advocated a fifth goal called prema (love of God) or nitya-seva (eternal loving service).

Still, most Hindus consider moksha the main aim of human life, toward which the others are incremental steps, adopted according to individual needs. Texts therefore recommend a balanced life with an ultimate spiritual goal. Liberation usually entails union with God, called 'yoga', and the various processes are therefore called yogas or, alternatively, margas ('paths').

DIFFERENT PATHS

There are three main paths: karma-yoga (the yoga of action), jnana-yoga (the yoga of wisdom), and bhakti-yoga (the yoga of devotion). Texts such as the Bhagavad-gita add a fourth called astanga-yoga (the yoga

Above A businessman worships Ganesha and Lakshmi online. Generating wealth is one of four 'aims of human life'.

of meditation). Within these four yogas exist many sub-disciplines, such as hatha-yoga, a stage within the path of meditation. Some traditions, such as the Shri Vaishnavas, consider their chosen path higher than the standard four.

There are different opinions as to the respective merits of each yoga. Some view all equally, like paths up a mountain or rivers merging into the ocean. Choice is determined by personal preference or disposition.

Above The loving exchanges between Vishnu and Lakshmi are esteemed by many following the devotional path.

Other traditions favour one process, citing the example of a ladder and claiming that each rung is a successive step toward the perfection achieved through their particular yoga. Despite the notion of successive stages, the yogas are not entirely separated, and the phases are cumulative, building on previous ones rather than rejecting them. For bhaktas, knowledge is a preliminary stage to the superlative path of devotion; for jnanis, devotion is an elementary process for those ill-equipped for the stringent path of knowledge.

ARE ALL PATHS THE SAME?

Some Hindu teachers, such as Ramakrishna, have recommended that all paths, including other faiths, lead to the same goal. He said, 'A truly religious man should think that other religions also are paths leading to truth'. Others suggest that different paths and processes yield different destinations. In the Bhagavad-gita, Krishna explains, 'Those who worship the demigods take birth among the demigods; those who worship the ancestors go to the ancestors; those who worship ghosts and spirits, take birth among such beings; and those who

worship me will live with me'. Despite differences of opinion, practically all agree on the need for maintaining an attitude of respect towards other religions. A related idea is that of concession, a belief that the individual has to act according to his or her present situation, and specific dharma (duty), even if not ideal. Moving in the right direction is preferable to attempting immediate perfection.

PURITY AND IMPURITY

Hindu teachings imply it is dangerous to be critical of others, even if their specific dharma is less prestigious, as this story illustrates.

Once there lived a very strict brahmin. He was upset that he lived next door to a prostitute, and was irked every time he spied her bringing home a customer. He decided to teach her a lesson. Every time she brought a client home, he lobbed a stone into her garden. As the months and years passed, the pile grew taller and wider. Whenever, the brahmin saw it, he would again be outraged at his neighbour's conduct.

The lady was also upset. Seeing the pile of stones, she would think, 'Due to my past impious activities, I have been engaged in this rotten business. But that brahmin next door is so pure. Oh, I wish I could be like him. Maybe later on, at least in the next life, I will get the opportunity to become saintly'. Although destiny engaged her in a lowly profession, the prostitute was actually a devotee of God.

Life went on. The brahmin thanked fate that he was not like others, particularly his neighbour. And the prostitute contemplated the purity of the brahmin and the trouble she was causing him. The pile of stones continued to grow.

Right Illustration conveying the view that the various yogas are progressive. This version favours bhakti (devotion).

Above Many non-Hindus identify yoga with hatha-yoga, the preliminary stages of the Hindu meditative path.

As fate decreed, both the brahmin and the prostitute passed away. Absorbed in thoughts of his neighbour's sins, the brahmin was born into a wretched and degraded family. The prostitute, aware of her own shortcomings and full of admiration for the brahmin, at once attained the heavenly planets.

Bhakti Yoga
Devotional service

Raja Yoga
Meditation

Jnana Yoga
Spiritual Knowledge

Karma Yoga
Selfless action

TIME AND SPACE

HINDU IDEAS ON TIME AND SPACE GIVE INSIGHT INTO ITS DISTINCTIVE
WORLD VIEW. BELIEF IN CYCLICAL TIME AND INTELLIGENT LIFE ON
OTHER PLANETS PROMOTES IDEAS OF RELIGIOUS INCLUSIVITY.

Hindu texts describe expanses of time and space so vast that some consider them fanciful. Traditional historic dates go back tens and hundred of millennia and, even when more recent, usually predate the estimates favoured by scholars. At the heart of this, Hindu versions of history differ from popular views. Traditional myth recalls a glorious heritage, with descent from highly refined rishis (saints), rather than evolutionary emergence from a tribal past.

Such belief is underpinned by Hindu views on time and space, which radically depart from contemporary belief. Time is eternal and cyclical rather than bounded and linear. Space accommodates life not just on earth, but on a multitude of lokas (worlds) occupying various metaphysical dimensions. Hindu cosmology thus suggests that knowledge of time and space is not entirely objective, but is influenced by the perceptive capacity of the transmigrating soul. Enlightenment, or realization of the true self, opens up levels of perception beyond common understanding.

TIME

The concept of eternal and cyclical time is intimately linked to core belief about the self. The atman is neither created nor destroyed. This notion of bi-directional eternity is not confined to the realm of spirit (Brahman) but extends to the material world. Hindu texts do not generally mention an absolute 'year dot' or a final cataclysm. Destruction of the cosmos inevitably heralds its re-creation.

The material cosmos is therefore subject to continuous cycles of creation, sustenance and annihilation, with each function overseen by one of three main deities, the 'Trimurti'. This cyclical idea differs from modern belief in unidirectional progress. On the contrary, Hindu texts describe universal and social devo-

Above Brahma, the creator, with his original five heads, as painted by a Western artist.

lution, with a gradual decline in human morality and wellbeing. This is likened to the shared human experience of physical atrophy, of always aging. However, the Hindu view is that, after steady decline, both the soul and the universe are periodically and rapidly rejuvenated through rebirth. Texts frequently draw such parallels between the universe (the macrocosm) and the physical body (the microcosm).

Left Vishnu emits universes from his pores and breath. Vaishnavas claim he oversees primary creation, with Brahma born in each universe as the 'secondary creator.'

THE FOUR AGES
Hindu notions of time reflect the rhythms of nature. There are four ages that continuously rotate, rather like the four seasons. They are:

Satya-yuga – 1,728,000 years
Dvapara-yuga – 1,296,000 years
Treta-yuga – 864, 000 years
Kali-yuga – 432,000 years

Total cycle – 4,320,000 years

CREATION HYMN

The following Purusha Shukta prayer of the Rig Veda illustrates the Hindu belief that the spiritual realm is larger than the material world.

Oh Lord, the past, present and future universe are creations of your powers. But you are much greater. This material word is only one-quarter of the entire cosmos. The eternal spiritual sky constitutes the remaining three-quarters.

This universe exists for the life-span of Brahma, the creator. His one day consists of 1,000 maha-yugas (great ages), each comprised of four yugas or ages: the golden, silver, copper and iron ages, each progressively shorter and more depraved. Tradition calculates that we now live 5,000 years into this Kali-yuga, with 427,000 years remaining. Some Hindu writers suggest a far shorter period. At the end of Kali-yuga, the final incarnation of Vishnu is scheduled to appear as Kalki, riding a white horse, slaying the sinful and ushering in yet another golden age.

SPACE

With a cyclical notion of time, Hinduism teaches that the material world is created not once but repeatedly. This universe is often considered to be one of many, which are compared to a cluster of bubbles floating in space. Within this universe are three main regions: the heavenly planets, the earthly realm and the lower worlds. Scripture provides detailed descriptions of these regions and their diversely shaped inhabitants. The idea of Indra's heaven, predominant in Vedic times, has

Right 19th-century diagram of the universe, showing its stratified and hierarchical nature.

more recently been augmented by the idea of an eternal realm, either as the brahman effulgence or as a fully equipped paradise, usually ruled by Vishnu or Shiva. Vaishnavism has developed this latter concept to embrace the notion of lila, or spiritual pastimes replicated within sacred locations on earth when Vishnu appears. Holy places have often been compared to spiritual embassies, or to fords and gateways that provide access to higher dimensions.

There is no one account of creation, but many inter-related stories. The Rig Veda narrates the story of the sacrifice of the primal being (purusha). According to Sankhya philosophy, the universe is created from sound (vach), represented by the Om mantra. Sound corresponds to ether, the subtlest of the five material elements, and the elements are generated successively from subtle to gross. In a manner that mirrors universal creation, the atman, more subtle and powerful than matter,

Above Shiva, Lord of the Dance, is often termed 'the destroyer'. Shaivas also consider Lord Shiva the ultimate re-creator and sustainer.

generates its own successive material bodies. This world facilitates the soul's various, self-centred desires, and ultimately brings him back to his pure spiritual identity as Brahman.

HINDU VALUES

TEXTS DO NOT DEAL ONLY WITH PHILOSOPHICAL AND THEOLOGICAL KNOWLEDGE. THEY INCLUDE MORAL GUIDELINES AND INJUNCTIONS TO REGULATE SOCIAL, MORAL AND SPIRITUAL CONDUCT.

Texts extensively list human virtues, such as humility, honesty and cleanliness. Hindu thought recognizes the interplay between values and belief, such as in the indestructible atman, and also between values and conduct, as regulated though dharma (duty and etiquette). The greeting of 'namaskara' or 'namaste', uttered with folded palms, is deeply embedded in Indian culture. Hindus use it to greet each other and their sacred images. In celestial social circles, the gods and goddesses use the same salutation, which literally means, 'I bow to you', but more profoundly, 'I bow to you, the eternal self within'. It is based on

Below This painting shows the pitfalls of the Kali age, and how Emperor Parikshit punished the personification of Kali for daring to enter his kingdom.

the foundational belief in both spiritual equality and a hierarchal world. The gesture also embodies specifically Hindu values, such as a humble respect for all. This simple practice reflects both philosophical ideas and spiritual values.

VALUES AND CONCEPTS

Belief in reincarnation has moulded specific attitudes toward issues surrounding the sanctity of life. For example, since the self apparently enters the body upon conception, many texts condemn abortion. More broadly, all life is seen in terms not of its physical symptoms, eating, breathing and reproduction, but its inherent capacity for consciousness, and for pleasure and pain. The Bhagavad-gita defines knowledge as awareness of the self in all life forms; conversely, ignorance as denial of the

Above A warrior pays respect to a brahmin. Members of these two varnas were expected to demonstrate lofty virtues, such as wisdom and nobility.

existence and feelings of others.

According to modern Hindu theology, moral issues are evaluated in terms of the three gunas, or 'material qualities'. Desirable values relate to sattva-guna, the quality of goodness. The quality of passion (rajo-guna), though essential for creative activities, is influenced by greed. The lowest quality of ignorance (tamo-guna) indicates immorality and, according to the Bhagavad-gita, a firm conviction that right is wrong and vice versa.

VALUES AND DHARMA

Values are linked to the execution of dharma (religious duties). Varnashrama is based on the notion that members of the four varnas are determined by their situation within the three gunas and their exhibition of corresponding characteristics. The authentic brahmin is meant to demonstrate goodness and hence serenity, wisdom and detachment. They effectively lead society through real knowledge, a serene and unbiased

perception of reality. The other varnas tend to be swayed by political, economic and sensual expediency.

Nevertheless, all varnas are regarded as important, and each is allocated distinctive values as stepping-stones toward ideal character. The values required of a business person are different from those required of a scholar, teacher or doctor, who fulfil brahminical functions. Whereas the business community is closely connected to money, the brahmins were traditionally prohibited from receiving a wage to avoid compromising their integrity and mood of public service. Brahmins were also responsible for education, which focused on character formation as much as earning a livelihood.

The varna system relates to ideas of internal and external purity. The degree of purity of the self or, conversely, of contamination by the three gunas, determines the soul's

Below Vishvamitra, though born a warrior, became a powerful brahmin. Here, the heavenly damsel Menaka tests his detachment.

Above Traditional Hindu education, as practised in this Swaminarayan School in London, stresses the importance of character formation.

destination at death. Ideas of ritual purity were exploitatively embedded in the hereditary caste system, by which higher classes avoid intimate contact – through eating, physical contact or marriage – with those of lower status. Such rigid practices have long been contested by reformers and devotional movements who stressed instead the spiritual equality of all people.

The notion of Sanatana Dharma supports the ideal of shared human values. Such virtues are not artificially imposed but nurtured from within through culture and spiritual discipline, including worship, austerity, and meditation. Hindu society emphasises the benefits of sadhu-sanga (or sat-sanga), keeping company with pious, saintly people. Hindus still show them respect by reverentially touching their feet and seeking their good wishes and blessings.

VALUES AND STORY
Story remains an essential means of transmitting values. How heroes and heroines embody key virtues is illustrated through their conduct. Many stories focus on the kshatriyas and brahmins, the two varnas most responsible for maintaining social

and spiritual culture. Hindu stories, such as the Mahabharata, often explore the difficulties in performing dharma and in distinguishing right from wrong under trying or unusual circumstances.

Proverbs and legend are other popular ways of nurturing character and wisdom. Moral instruction is found in Niti Shastra texts, like those written by Chanakya. Also popular are legends that have grown around various key figures such as Birbal, the chief minister of the Mughal Emperor Akbar. More recently, some view Mahatma Gandhi as a champion not only of Hindu values but also of modern egalitarian thought. However, traditional Hinduism also challenges modern liberal and libertarian values by stressing the need for sensual and sexual restraint. In Hindu terms, this indicates the degraded nature of this age, the Kali-yuga, which is typified by hypocrisy and quarrelling, and a lack of four key virtues: honesty, austerity, cleanliness and compassion.

GLOSSARY

ADVAITA non-dualism; the philosophy that the soul and God are identical

AGAMAS Tantric texts, not directly Vedic; many have been assimilated into more orthodox traditions

AHIMSA non-violence, a core Hindu virtue, as taught by Gandhi

ALVARS South Indian, early-medieval poet-saints who worshipped Vishnu and sang in the Tamil language

ANTARYAMI God living within the heart and guiding all living beings

ANUMANA inference, or knowledge based on reasoning

ARATI a popular Hindu ceremony in which auspicious articles, including a camphor lamp, are offered to the murti

ARTHA economic development, one of the four aims of human life

ARYA SAMAJ a principal 19th-century reform movement

ARYAN 'noble people', those with spiritual values; European scholars considered Aryans a specific race

ASHRAMA a place where spirituality is cultivated; one of the four stages in life

ASTANGA-YOGA the eightfold meditational path culminating in samadhi (trance). One of the four main paths

ASURAS the demons, who are powerful but impious beings, constantly fighting with the gods (the Devas)

ATMAN literally 'self', it ultimately refers to the soul

BENGALI VAISHNAVAS (Gaudiya Vaishnavas) the followers of Chaitanya

BHAGAVAD-GITA the 'Song of God', the text spoken by Krishna to Arjuna

BHAGAVAN literally 'possessing all opulence'; a popular word for God; also used for some saints

BHAGAVAT PURANA one of the major Puranas, containing the famous stories of Krishna

BHAJANA adoration with song, chanting, and so on; a hymn

BHAKTI the path of devotional service; one of the four main paths

BRAHMA the four-headed deity in charge of creation

BRAHMACHARIN a celibate student, member of the first stage of life

BRAHMAN the absolute and all-pervading reality

BRAHMANAS one of four main divisions of text in the Vedas

BRAHMIN (or brahmana) a member of the highest varna; a priest, teacher or intellectual

BRAHMINISM (or Brahmanism) the orthodox strand of Hinduism supervised by brahmins

BRAHMO SAMAJ a 19th-century reform movement

CHAKRA Vishnu's disk weapon, also called Sudarshana; an energy centre in Tantric-yoga

DALIT 'the oppressed', or 'schedules classes', outcastes, previously called the untouchables

DARSHANA 'seeing', the act of taking audience of a deity; also, 'perspective', referring to six orthodox Hindu philosophies

DEVI 'goddess', most often referring to the consort of Shiva

DHARMA religious duties that sustain humans and the universe

DIVALI the well-known festival of lights, coinciding for many Hindus with their New Year

DRAVIDIAN 'from the South', in contrast to the north often linked to the Aryans

DVAITA dualism, the theology that the soul and God are different, especially as taught by Madhva

GAYATRI a mantra of 24 syllables chanted thrice daily by Brahmins

GITA song; an abbreviated form of 'Bhagavad-gita'

GOPURAM a lofty South Indian temple gateway, often adorned with figurines

GUNA literally 'rope', one of the three qualities that control matter

GURU a spiritual teacher

HAVANA (or Homa) the sacred fire ceremony of Vedic times

HINDU MAHASABHA political party, a forerunner to many nationalistic movements

HOLI spring festival in which participants douse each other with dyes and coloured water

ISHVARA literally 'ruler' or 'controller', it refers to God or any male deity. The feminine form is Ishvari

ISKCON The International Society for Krishna Consciousness, popularly known as the Hare Krishna Movement

JAPA the meditational practice of reciting mantras silently or quietly on prayer beads

JATI occupational sub-group within each of the four varnas

JNANA knowledge; jnana-yoga is the path of wisdom, one of the four main paths

KALI-YUGA the fourth age, the age of iron or the age of quarrel

KAMA sensual gratification, especially sex; regulated sensory pleasure is one of the four aims of life

KARMA literally 'action'; often used to mean 'reaction', or the accumulated stock of such reactions

KIRTANA 'glorification', usually referring to the musical chanting of mantras

KSHATRIYA 'one who protects', a member of the second varna, the warrior class

KUMBHA MELA 'The pot-fair', a huge triennial bathing festival

LILA the transcendental, sporting activities of some deities

MAHA great, as in Mahatma, meaning 'great soul'

MANDIR temple, the home of the sacred image

MANU SMRITI the 'codebook for mankind', ascribed to Manu; an ancient text dealing with morality

MATAJI 'respected mother', a form of address for any lady or goddess; in the south, 'Amma' or 'Ammachi'

MIMAMSA literally 'reverential enquiry'; one of the Six Darshanas

MOKSHA liberation from samsara, the cycle of repeated birth and death

MUNI a sage, or deep thinker

MURTI literally 'form', it specifically refers to the sacred image

NAVARATRI literally 'nine-nights', a nine-day festival in honour of Devi

NAYANMARS the 63 Shaiva poet-saints of southern India

NYAYA logic, one of the six orthodox schools (Darshanas)

OM (Aum) the most important Hindu mantra, of three syllables

PADMA lotus, a key symbol used to denote beauty e.g. 'lotus eyes'. It is symbolic of beauty and purity

PITHA literally 'seat', a Shakta holy site; a holy seat belonging to the various religious schools

PITRI the forefathers; during Vedic times, Hindus aspired to reach pitriloka, the world of the ancestors

PRAKRITI material energy, in contrast to eternal brahman; it consists of three tendencies or qualities

PRASADA God's 'mercy'; secondarily, it refers to any item sanctified by offering to God, especially food

PRATYAKSHA direct perception, one key source of evidence

PUJA ritualistic worship, most often of the installed murti

PUJARI the temple priest, who performs the puja

PURANA 'very old'; the texts containing many popular and ancient religious stories

PURI flat bread fried in oil or ghee; also a holy town in East India

PURUSHA person, specifically male; refers to the soul or to God

PUSHTI MARG 'the path of nourishment', a Vaishnava lineage started by the saint called Vallabha

RAJA 'king' or 'kingly'; maharaja literally means 'great king'

RAJO-GUNA (or Rajas) second of the three material qualities; the royal quality of passion or ambition

RAKSHA BANDHANA festival in which sisters tie a rakhi (bracelet) on the wrists of their brothers

RAMAYANA 'the journey of Rama'; the earlier of the two Hindu Epics, composed in Sanskrit by Valmiki

RANGOLI a pattern made by Hindu women and girls; also called 'kolam' in Tamil, Rangavalli in Sanskrit

RASA-LILA the divine dance that Krishna performs with his girl-friends, the gopis (cowherd girls)

RIG VEDA the foremost and possibly earliest of the four Vedas

RISHI sage or seer, usually from ancient times

RITA 'the natural order', an important concept during the Vedic period

RUDRAKSHA berry from which Shaiva prayer beads are made

SADHU a saintly person; often refers to sannyasins, members of fourth ashrama

SAMADHI 'fixed mind', the final perfect stage of meditational yoga; also the tomb of a saint

SAMHITA one of four sections of the Vedas; also the name of some Tantric texts

SAMPRADAYA a disciplic succession, or lineage, of gurus and disciples teaching spiritual knowledge

SAMSARA the perpetual cycle of birth and death; the process of suffering on account of this

SAMSKARA literally 'mental impression', referring to a sacrament or rite of passage

SANATANA DHARMA 'the eternal religion', the eternal function of the soul; often preferred to the more recent term 'Hinduism'

SANGAM 'gathering', specifically ancient South Indian conventions; also refers to the ancient Tamil literature

SANKHYA one of the six darshans, it analyses matter in detail and also identifies the atman

SANSKRIT 'the most refined language', the sacred tongue of Hinduism

SANSKRITIZATION a process by which village gods and practices are elevated to 'high', scholarly Hinduism

SANT saint, especially of the northern, esoteric and eclectic devotional tradition from 1200CE onwards

SATTVA-GUNA the highest of the three material qualities, characterized by serenity

SATYA 'truth'; satyagraha, a term coined by Gandhi, means 'adhering to truth'

SHABDA sound, also referring to scripture as a source of reliable evidence

SHAKTAS the worshippers of Shakti

SHAKTI a generic term to refer to the female deity, especially the consort of Shiva

SHASTRA literally 'that which commands'; scripture, used particularly of some texts e.g. the dharma-shastras

SHRAMANISM the anti-social renouncer traditions, in contrast to orthodox Brahmanism

SHRI VAISHNAVAS one of four main Vaishnava sampradayas, founded by Ramanuja and others and popular in South India

SHRUTI that which has been heard'; one of two main sections of Vedic texts

SHUDRA a member of the fourth varna, an artisan or labourer

SMARTAS one of the four main denominations; members worship five or six deities

SMRITI 'that which is remembered', the second broad category of Hindu texts

SOMA a celestial intoxicant used in Vedic sacrifice; also the moon

SUTRA literally 'thread'; an aphorism that can be spun out indefinitely to reveal ever-fresh insight

SVETASHVATARA UPANISHAD one of the Upanishads, canonical for many Shaivas

SWAMI 'master' or 'controller'; a title used for sannyasis, who must control their senses

SWAMINARAYANA MISSION a Vaishnava sampradaya, popular among Gujarati Hindus

TAMAH-GUNA (or Tamas) lowest of the three material qualities, typified by darkness, laziness and ignorance

TANTRA strand of Hinduism, and texts, stressing esoteric discipline based on complementary male–female energies

TILAK a clay mark applied to the forehead, denoting the wearer's denominational affiliation.

TIRTHA literally 'ford'; a holy place

TRIMURTI the three main deities, Brahma (creator), Vishnu (sustainer) and Mahesh, or Shiva (the destroyer)

TULASI a plant of the basil family, sacred to Vaishnavas who use the leaf for worship and the wood for beads

UPANISHAD philosophical texts identified with Vedanta and one of four sections of the Vedas

UPAVEDAS four texts, supplementary to the Vedas and explaining traditional arts and sciences

VAISHNAVAS worshippers of Vishnu or one of his forms or avatars

VAISHYA a member of the third varna, the farming and mercantile community

VARNA the largest social unit, originally based on disposition but now usually on birth

VARNASHRAMA-DHARMA social system with different duties allocated to four classes and four stages in life

VEDA literally 'knowledge'; the Vedas are the four main Shruti texts at the heart of Hindu literature

VEDANGAS texts supplementary to the four Vedas

VEDANTA 'the conclusion of the Vedas', one of the six darshanas, representing much modern thought in Hinduism

VEDANTA SUTRA an important, philosophical section of the Smriti literature

VEDIC 'connected to, or derived from, the Vedas'. Also, 'linked to the period when the Vedas were compiled'

VISHNU, one of the Trimurti, the sustainer

YAJNA 'ritual sacrifice', as prevalent during the Vedic age but still performed through the havan

YAMA moral restrictions; also the God of Death, 'one who controls'; positive moral observances are called 'niyama'

YANTRA a geometrical diagram connected to meditational Tantra

YOGA union with the Supreme, or any practice aimed at self or God realization

YOGI one who performs yoga; the feminine is 'yogini'

FURTHER READING

A.C. Bhaktivedanta Swami Prabhupada, *Bhagavad-Gita As It Is* (Bhaktivedanta Book Trust, 2002)

William Buck, *Ramayana* (University of California Press, 2000)

Christopher Chapple, *Yoga and the Luminous* (State University of New York Press, 2008)

Rasamandala Das, *Atlas of World Faiths: Hinduism* (Franklin Watts, 2007)

Rasamandala Das, *The Heart of Hinduism* (ISKCON Educational Services, 2002)

Krishna Dharma, *The Mahabharata* (Torchlight, 1999)

Gavin Flood, *An Introduction to Hinduism* (Cambridge University Press, 1996)

Anita Ganeri and Rasamandala Das, *Hindu Prayer and Worship* (Franklin Watts, 2006)

Sue Hamilton, *A Very Short Introduction to Indian Philosophy* (Oxford University Press, 2000)

Linda Johnsen, *The Complete Idiot's Guide to Hinduism* (Alpha, 2002)

Klaus K. Klostermaier, *Hinduism: A Short History* (One World, 2006)

Klaus K. Klostermaier, *A Survey of Hinduism* (State University of New York Press, 2007)

Kim Knott, *A Very Short Introduction to Hinduism* (Oxford University Press, 2000)

Gwyneth Little, *Meeting Hindus* (Christians Aware, 2002)

Ranchor Prime, *Vedic Ecology* (Mandala Publishing, 2002)

Hillary Rodriguez, *Introducing Hinduism* (Routledge, 2006)

INDEX